The Work of the Sun

Other Books by Charles Edward Eaton

Poetry
The Bright Plain
The Shadow of the Swimmer
The Greenhouse in the Garden
Countermoves
On the Edge of the Knife
The Man in the Green Chair
Colophon of the Rover
The Thing King
The Work of the Wrench
New and Selected Poems, 1942–1987
A Guest on Mild Evenings
The Country of the Blue
The Fox and I
The Scout in Summer
The Jogger by the Sea
Beneath the Devil and the Deep Blue Sea

Short Stories
Write Me from Rio
The Girl from Ipanema
The Case of the Missing Photographs
New and Selected Stories, 1959–1989

Novel
A Lady of Pleasure

Critical Biography
Karl Knaths: Five Decades of Painting

Autobiographical and Critical Essays
The Man from Buena Vista: Selected Nonfiction, 1944–2000

The Work of the Sun

New and Selected Poems, 1991–2002

Charles Edward Eaton

Cornwall Books
Cranbury, NJ

Cornwall Books
2010 Eastpark Boulevard
Cranbury, New Jersey 08512

The paper used in this publication meets the requirements of the American National Standard for Permanence of Paper for Printed Library Materials Z39.48-1984.

Acknowledgments:

Permission to reprint the new poems from the following sources is hereby acknowledged. *Carolina Quarterly:* "The Wheatfield," "The Crisis in the Icecream," "Kangaroo," and "The Etymologist in the Orchard", *Chariton Review:* "Swan in Search of the City"; *Chattahoochee Review:* "Cauldron"; *Chronicles:* "Zebra" and "Clean Sweep"; *The New Criterion:* "The Work of the Sun"; *New Letters:* "Fallen Arches" and "Hourglass"; *Pembroke Magazine:* "Choke Collar," and "Atlas In the Evening"; *Salmagundi:* "The Navel Gazer," "The Luge," "Deep Breathing at Midnight," and "Cameo"; *The Wallace Stevens Journal:* "The Lever."

Library of Congress Cataloging-in-Publication Data

Eaton, Charles Edward, 1916–
   The work of the sun : new and selected poems, 1991–2002 / Charles Edward Eaton.
     p. cm.
   ISBN 0-8453-4887-6 (alk. paper)
   I. Title.
   PS3509.A818W58   2004
   811'.54—dc22   2003016968

To Isabel

Contents

The Country of the Blue (1994)

The Jogger by the Sea (2002)

The Work of the Sun

*A Guest
on Mild Evenings* (1991)

He who succeeds in reconciling the many contradictions of his life, holding them all together in a symbol, pushes the noisy crowd from the palace and will be festive in a different sense, receiving you as his guest on mild evenings.

—Rainer Maria Rilke

I

The Lynx

We draw our lives after ourselves in streams—
The hurly-burly, the raw, rough, the long silken passage,
The lynx poised on the rock above, the bathing girl of our high
    dreams.

Those creamy, creamy shoulders and the brilliant, piercing eyes,
The suntanned skin, the tawny fur, the tension of the leap—
Who told you beauty and the beast could never share the selfsame
    paradise?

Do not think that these associations do not come and go—
The woman with her long, blood-red fingernails, lethal too,
The lynx, purring, pensive, turned albino, changed in the mind,
    soft as snow.

The woman, rising in the rift, streams and streams with gold:
We keep on making up her myth, holding, holding, setting stasis
    on the cat,
As if we would not run the risk, rupture that quietus, until the
    story, manifold, is told.

The lynx will keep his amber tone, her breasts are almond-white—
See how the mind goes back and forth with just two figures to
    control:
Think how the dam will slack and overflow when we lie down at
    night.

We stream and stream, push on, ahead, beyond—
I only tell you this because the lady with the blood-red nails may
    one day dive
Where the spill has left the maw of all reflection yawning in the
    pond.

The Stretcher

A soldier who looks like yourself is sprawled
Out naked on a bed of violets.
All of the wounds of war have passed him by;
His helmet is the home of daffodils,
His clothes spread like a fail-safe parachute.
He is tan, looks cleaned by the sun's strigil.
Nestled, the green grass like hair on his legs,
He is the most accomplished accoucheur.

She comes with her sun hat, picnic basket,
To find the love-child the wars of life have spared.
Her dimpled smile, breast full as a wine jug,
Are just the reparations for the raptor:
Let the fruit roll on the ground and her clothes
Be flung at the foot of the well-known soldier—
It is as though a dank tomb of the mind
Has opened like a mouth lined with flowers.

This is how one speaks on those days when one
Is counting causes and catastrophes,
Dreaming white crosses and fields of poppies,
Each piercing sorrow borne on a stretcher.
The lovely girl looks bandaged in her clothes,
The home casualties and the fires burning—
Someone rushes roses into the room,
And ideas pass each other like interns.

Therefore, look and look for the overlooked,
The flamingo that flicks from the bloodshot eye,
The ripe melons that are dropped by the sun,
The rough sea that sometimes waves a white flag—

You are wedging, here, there, at least a wish:
A frayed rope that holds as the climber falls,
How the fangs of the snake can miss their mark,
The windshield held fast in its broken veins.

So for a moment you are shuttled there—
Someone, something, has carried you away,
The naked soldier on the violet bank.
There are those who hate the just so carried,
Not knowing that the wink can wage its wars,
The bird from the eye bear up the lover.
Just as the corpse corners the stretcher,
The sway of the hammock will let it go.

The Axle

Sometimes he thought that it would bring him down,
The sense of the axle, the inward shaft,
As if he were upended on a wheel,
The whirling dome filled with amoretti
As though desire had ditched him in this place.
He might have known there was much too much grease
When, horizontal, he gripped the beloved,
Leaned back and stained the antimaccassar,
And knew he had turned some great lode of love.
Sometimes, nude on the beach, it came on him
That he had gotten this far and was stalled,
The sea's sapphire impenetrable to wheels,
The ripe fallen fruit looking like boulders—
The metallic thrust bent and no anvil.
Then why not simply let it turn itself,
The amoretti circling, the catching up,
The girl hitching a ride into your dream,
Even the sea opening up its rifts
As if, despite you, chariots rode on,
The continuous carousel of clouds—
More often than you think it comes to this,
The stationary stance, the lush spinning,
The streaked oil on the face that spoils the kiss,

The hard, bruised feet in the sea of sapphires,
The bunions bulging in a contest checked,
This sense of upright rod and stymied wheel—
In this land of chipped diamonds and no mire,
No saving grace of having rutted down:
The turning like a bit into that blue,
The thrown spear of sex lodged in a sand dune—
You wait and wait, she catches up with you,
Your head comes down into a groove. You turn,
Blent like an axle in each other's arms.
One notices the clouds have stopped, the sea
Has flattened out its long, jeweled road.
Earth, too, admires this rare, rolling splendor—
We feel its axis running through the heart.

The Summerhouse

One has this vision of the summerhouse when the peonies bloom:
White, latticed at the eaves, a romance of the past,
It conjures lovers who are looking for a mortal and immortal
    room.

It takes a hint from pink, and, there beyond—flamingo lake.
Those mortal birds that look so posed and so contrived
Are wading in a world in which our lovers want a stake.

They want the peony-blush, the brilliant feather, and the bluest
    sky—
Yesterday they ate their half a loaf and threw the crust away,
And they have come here, in extravagance, expecting crumbs to
    multiply.

How can one say to her: Not quite, not absolutely all, my dear—
Tomorrow the selfsame loaf upon the selfsame table,
The dying strains of *liebestod* in your lover's ruddy ear.

One cannot say it yet because one also wants the whole—
An athlete of desire has flung the peony like a shot expanding:
Here the summerhouse, and there flamingos wading in the soul.

The famished heart, the flinging—the idea of the Idea of whole
    bread—
The rumps of flowers ruffle in the wind where the shot puts down:
I listen, listen to the splashing in the water, and then the silent
    tread.

The Glioma

No matter how beautiful the morning,
There was a weight like a gallstone harbored
For years. Even the geysers of good will
Left silt, a certain gas in the nostrils.

If he were a goldeneye duck, he would
Drop from the mass of his vision.
A fob on his vest could tip the balance;
Lover's beads on his cheek were a warning,

The gardenia she brushed across his lips
A subtle blow—just that little extra.
Must he, in fact, wear a gas mask against
Her perfume, the scent of violets turning to stone?

Toward night he could feel rapt, like Harlequin
In purple suit with whipped cream collar, cuffs,
Begging mirrors not to add their shadows
As if reflections give the coup de grâce.

Where was the goblet to hold his sputum,
Heavy as liquid rubies in the mouth?—
Urine must come from a topaz fountain;
Passing a stone would gem a lovely hand.

If the west wind blew too hard, he could sit
On flapping landscape like a paperweight.
Should he enter an oscillating room
He would curb, calm, it like a gyroscope.

One day he might extract a single gold tooth,
Secret, hidden in the back of his mouth,

And the glioma would begin to heal,
Lifting like a balloon dragging its ballast.

You know those sunlit, light, and lofty days—
Harlequin stands on his head, drops his grief;
A lover's long beads release their gallows—
The chip on the shoulder flutters its wings.

The Great Chain of Being

The man had paintings, jewels, a house called *Nonpareil,*
A pool like a Sultan's sapphire infinitely enlarged,
A garden that gleamed and quivered with exquisite specimens.

All of this in a dream, mind you, all of it in a world that would
        never be—
The courtesan who had been heightened from a call girl
Had a name and nature made up by him of careful steppingstones.

What did it matter if all that he had was a pocket full of glass
Picked up on the beach, spilled from the till of the waves,
When he was such a lapidary they would lie on velvet before
        nightfall?

Do I need to elaborate this magical study of happiness?—
A man for whom each image was immanent and imbedded, for
Whom the gods indeed had hung down the earth on a golden
        chain.

He could see it, in miniature, in a gold fob that he coveted,
The voluptuous relaxation of it in a pendant in a jeweler's window,
The rope pull that would ring the bells, the knob and tassel that
        he could carry home.

Ah, such gravity, the world hanging, swaying everywhere,
Ready to drop into his hand, the ecstasy, the reaching for
        rondure—
The spasm when a single thing he loved dropped into the abyss.

26

Those of us who own a watch, a bracelet, a pair of teardrop
    earrings.
Know a little of desire's dependence, how a tug, a shift in the wind,
    a clasp undone
Threatens to scatter in the darkness the full, firm pouch of
    substance.

Pull a thread and the whole rich dress ravels endlessly.
A man in his socks and garters feels all too lightly hung,
A lifeline flung to a golden swimmer brings in the reamed-out
    bathing suit.

Thus even in sleep the great, coiled, glimmering ball and chain—
Nevertheless, it would not be wise to altogether lighten, throw
    away the world:
A ring, a fob, perhaps, but can we, nestled in figments, heave down
    the heart and count on it to hold?

The Leash

Just the sweet taste of the rind—you were caught
By the pink tongue and were led by kumquats—
Just one of the many tugs the day would hold,
A hook in the nose from some rich perfume,
The gleam of a nude that pulled like a rope.
You may have shackles around your ankles,
But the arms reach out: take me to paradise.
Something lifts your head from the lavabo—
It is only the phone shrilly ringing:
I am waiting on the other side of town,
I have your only pedigree in hand,
And my time stretches only just so far—
Therefore, rings, tight collars, belts are suspect,
Recall the calendar of appointments.
It is easier to go than to stay.
That lesson was learned when you had the kite
In hand—it never wanted you to stop
In one place, and you ran long, stumbled,
And saw a blue ghost fluttering on the ground,
Nowhere's string gathered in a cat's cradle.

I know only a few who can solve it
In an eccentric way, poling their weight
Beneath them as they stand in a punt
Loaded with a girl, some cushions, ripe fruit,
As if last things of life were smaller in number.
You may have seen these mini-masters move,
Pushing the carcass of contentment on,
The water lilies like river sores healing.
Only this—with back turned, one did not count
On twinges, twitches, brushed by a sudden branch.
I have seen, in dreams, the boat and cargo
As if led by a leash, the man clinging
To the pole like a vaulter without bar
And only the rich river to sprawl on—
In this lacuna, one tastes the kumquat,
Savoring the synapses of sorrow,
Finding some joy in the lure of the line.

Truffles

When we become inhibited, when we are stalled and bound,
When style that opened all the doors has closed them,
We fold the brilliant heavens like a fan and think of going
    underground.

The peacock vanes of vision do not open anymore—
We have heard that there are luxuries, not too deep down,
    somewhere in the world,
And, with our fantail lust, we could take ship or plane for Périgord.

But, as we look at maps, consider schedules, funds, sitting at our
    desk,
Some lovely lady hung with pearls and iridescent webs
May say: At home we still spread out the riches of the earth in
    arabesque.

Touché. And when she stands in evening light so spread,
I call home all the ravaged cohorts of my style

To ask when, why, and just what went wrong in that authoritative
    campaign in my head.

This is the desperate time we call the truffle hound and pig,
Ready to go snuffling, snorting, rooting through the woods
To see, on this Atlantic side, if there is any overlooked and precious
    thing to dig.

By just this lust, perhaps, by going down to earth, each man
Turns up the brown potato-shapes like tubers of his style,
And she is standing in a better light, another image from that
    folded fan.

Bayou

It must be subtle, deep, and very close,
This love of secret waters, this tribute
To sleek waterbirds, the houses on stilts,
The sun like the largest jewel in the world
Enchased by a thick filigree of trees.
There must be time to read hands over
And over, the canals of the fingerprints
Themselves, showing the meandering course.
The great river pushed, gave us this largesse,
Or so it seems as we feel our rich veins,
Those of us devoted to the water trade—
Wondering how small a boat can ply the hand,
The tongue of a bird, a plectrum of song,
The house as pliant as a floating plant:
This extravagance of a corollary.
One needs a sideline to these summer days
When the streets seem filled with fierce amalgam.
There must be a place where they offer breasts
Like fruit and the cool water barely moves,
Where a soft eye is the only flashbulb
And you are pictured in a parish of peace.
Some may find it just as well in shaded backstreets,
Capping the primal scream with a caged bird,
The hand over the mouth and the barred song.

The prisoner remembers the smudged, blurred prints
As though these funicles could be redeemed—
Some day the bird and the long, gleaming thread!
All this one day when I pulled to the side
Of the road, let the cars go down the rush hour—
Indulge, indulge me with your sticky hands.
I would like your sinuous print upon me,
I would like the close bond of the bayou.
Let me be your first and last encomiast
As though we shared a ravishment so rare
Two boats are passing in the fine canals.

II

Eyewitness

Now close the lid of the blue pool, strangle
The geraniums, those doused, limp, red rags:
The body, flaking gold, will silver down.
One looks in the mirror for the bronze breastplate
Lost somewhere in that dung-brown pile of leaves.
There is this sense of the large, slow eye movement,
The mopping-up operation in red,
The demystification of the hero
Who looks white, hung up in his socks, locked in,
Having escaped the eye before it closed.
It may not even be autumn—just a loss
Of something you have greatly loved, that makes
The hand scratch at the exoskeleton,
Buff off the hard chairs with the old blood cloths,
Feeling the eyelid closing on the chest.
I give this précis to the passionate,
Those rubbed down often by the lens, who see
Their underwear go red in the bathroom,
Stand on the scales to weigh strange, base metal,
Clutching the fistula of another phase.
They will have dreams of hooks that lift the lid,
The rapt erections of geraniums,
The immense mining of a handsome bronze—
They know clear, bright morning best, however,
When the hydraulics are stalled—the slit eye,

Falling and forced open, bloodshot and clear,
Sees due process offered to the heart.

Among the Amazons

With the long, blonde hair coiled upon her head, the handsome
        stride,
Is there something in her person, a myth concealed,
Does all this flowing confidence have anything to hide?

Was it long ago somewhere she built up her effects,
All the boys killed at birth, the men driven in the woods—
Invited back to dine—just this once—on sex?

One could ask this of some man, that snorkeler there—
Why on this great, glorious, blue-flung day should he choose
To prowl below, and through the black, upright tube take in air?

People often seem so planted, delved into the past—
Does the man know some grotto for the image of the dominant
        male,
Is there a place where gold and silver figures with their shining
        breasts are cast?

The trouble came, of course, the day a cannibal remained,
Fell in love, but still was fitful in embrace
When there in the brilliant clearing he could see a man-child
        brained.

Everything so simple, cut and dried, out front, nothing in
        arrears—
I hardly can believe the slipped montage, the woman looking back
To see the one who dined, standing in his wetsuit, dripping tears.

Dead End

The avenue of trees, the violet light—
The spine felt pricked by a compass needle—
Was I stuck with the end of that blue day,
Having used the whole sea as an eye cup,
Winced down to a bucket, a grain of sand?—
One last splash for the Cyclops' heavy head
As if, to save itself, vision centered,
Found refuge in the beleaguered forehead.
Therefore, no mirrors on the long way back
That show the beach of the deserted sea:
Blue hulls everywhere as if the depths were skinned,
The great stone lighthouse grotesquely phallic—
It is afternoon, the blinkers at last,
The eyeshade over a single passion,
The light deepening, violet, then purple.
I must follow the fireflies if need be
And listen for wheels in the ruts of dusk—
Have these trees been groped much too much before
Like a stale mistress with the lights turned off,
The odors of old happiness everywhere?—
Blundering against the dropped picnic basket
Where the bottles pour out the last blue wine,
One fumbles at the head for a searchlight—
There is a hare trembling far down the road,
His two eyes glittering like life-enamored jewels—
This is for you when you can stand no more.
The eyes of the animal relieve the sea:
You can hear it now murmuring, murmuring,
Filling buckets, the enormous eye cup,
Looking for such gems on the inland road.
The rabbit hops off, I taste the sea air,
Long to see a blue tongue in a mirror—
We will repeat the same seizure often,
The evening with its narrowing, violet point—
A cummerbund across the central eye—
In these parts, one cannot hope for gazelles,
But you and I will not forget those jewels,
How they sang to the sea to save us all.

In Xanadu

So it was necessary to dress suitably, even wear a cat's-eye on a
    finger
As a sign to the day that all was not irremediably lost
Though even the rainbow had fallen around him like a tangled
    parachute—

This sense of his own iridescence in suffocating embrace:
No longer a brilliant arch—a tent always reducing itself
As it declared its intentions of becoming a shroud.

Friends began to notice that he could exclude them with a glance,
A roundabout way of looking that set a boundary: Just there—
Á trois, á deux, seul: stage directions for solitude.

Still, there was always a flutter underneath the shimmering cloth
As if a cocoon did somewhat regret its dispersal,
A flapping in the wind like the wings of a punctured balloon.

No one should ever claim too much for fallen rainbows,
Too moist with sentiment to dry piecemeal like confetti
One could throw to the winds in a romantic gala of freedom.

We can lie in bed and feel a renewed swollen swathe like a boa
    constrictor—
Some sex, some force of money, even a splurge in unknown,
    unused animal spirits—
Coil round and round until the constrained body floats another
    dream,

That exhalation upward with its bright, umbrageous canopy—
I describe, I think, a very common notion of decline and fall.
There was not enough, too much, an Adonic figure with a needle.

The idea of an impenetrable structure comes sooner than we
    think.
Even the futurists can love this daunting picture,
The plastic bubble on the moon where we grow our lives anew.

I remember the friend who one day dropped me off
Outside the curtain of those lovely, lucid colors:
Too little, or too much, I did not fit inside his pleasure dome.

So back to bed in some old hotel, the violent thrashings of the
    snake:
The good suit, the cat's-eye when I rise, a look that curves and
    curves—
So grandiose to think that it could hold in place the drifting and
    uncertain sky.

The Aborigine

At the onset of abulia, summon
The aborigine, the original
Landscape not yet erased by human eyes.
He will turn your stale mattress to fresh boughs,
A berry will taste like the earth's sweet blood;
Your gut will be a pocket for treasures,
Everything stroked and grasped at the same time,
Textures lining the nerves for the future.
Then the problem of placing arises:
A thatched triangle and posts—a hut.
Even without walls, the first garbage dump
Will now become a possibility.
In protest the aborigine dreams
The world as small as an orange he can eat,
Swallows the seeds for replanting, his dung
The soil of innumerable white blossoms.
Look through your own sleek conceptual skin—
From such red tissue you have rouged your thoughts.
There's a red spot in your cheeks when you kiss.
Some even let their hair flame in public;
Others go to war and smear the green fields;
A few, too stuffed with their own rubescence,
Leak into the hands of their psychiatrist.
He stands to wash away the interview,
Soaped by the lurid entrails of the pictures—
Just then the aborigine will knock
At the door, the shy, ultimate patient.
He will hand the good doctor an orange—
You know these bowers where we want to meet.

We have eaten with the same pair of lips:
Regurgitation, of course, comes later.

Quetzal

This raconteur of everything and nothing
Was sitting in his chair—
Was it the Mumm's he drank sometimes
Or the rotgut
Which made the blackbird on the fence
Burnish like a quetzal there?

It thrilled him so,
Ran up his backbone with such force—
His soul was cresting,
Spreading glittering wings: The raffish
And the raffiné—
How could he trace such plumage to its source?

He took another sip—
Whatever came to hand—
Remembered the dying chieftain, how the bird
Settled on his blood-stained chest
And in that instant somehow contrived
The brilliant from the bland.

Up into the trees
The breast the color of bright blood!—
I talk the matter over—
This time it must be Mumm's—
The best, the best—One cannot hail the bird
With drink that smells like urine, tastes like mud.

Still, deep down, both drinks share
A steady iridescent glow—
The raconteur is sometimes swamped
Among his many anecdotes:
I cannot always tell my own best friend
How much, just why, or what I know.

Worse or better—drinking nothing
But the air and light?—
The scarlet breast, the green, the glitter—
The legendary tellers say it does not matter
How it comes about, the rising in the spine,
The quetzal from the bird of night.

Home Thoughts from Abroad

We eat, drink, sweat, ride, kick the ball, play tennis,
Bathe to make love, and while we shower, think:
The gondolas are rotting in Venice.

Why should we acquire a style, why should we presume,
When the stirred sea breathes in our deep, veiled places?—
We think of acid rain in Florence, Rome.

If we look hard enough, pictures play upon the ceiling—
The summoned sea keeps tempting, as it discourages us, to thrive:
When was the last time you allowed yourself to live within a palace
    of fine feeling?

What suave animals we are—how the shower laves, licks our
    flesh!—
Our natural pauses, soft concussions, tug the long, interminable
    rope
As if we pulled the gondola to our knees to feel the parting mesh.

Is the world everywhere corrupt at last, an overwhelming melted
    mixture?—
One puts on a jockstrap, suits up, one pulls the rope:
Night comes. Is that black water with gleaming lights in all our
    moods a permanent fixture?

What busybodies, yet beautiful, so harlequin of mind, what ruth!—
Let us have coffee, comic songs, dancers by the glittering fountain,
And tell ourselves we have the duty? right? to practice on ourselves
    experiments with truth.

The Grommet

Having eaten the grapes, you are loaded,
Pointed toward life, ready to spew,
As if a mouth full of seed blows grapeshot,
And irradiation has the green light—
You do not want a grommet on your life,
You want the snake charmer, the head lifting,
Hypnotic and heavy, waiting to dart,
The sinuous system leaping toward hurdles—
There are many ways to tell this to the world.
Some sit for hours at low tide by the sea
Until the waves jumble their words, piling up
On the beach sprung pages from a blue book—
Others inhabit the thicket just to thrash
Their hard way out into open ground.
All some need is a tight cummerbund
To make them dance and dance the night away
As if rhythm itself wore a bellyband
And the lush earth shimmied in a girdle—
I, too, have thus held myself in a bit,
Locked oars for the night by the calm blue lake,
Matching breakfast orange with the rising sun,
Wondering if this day could be freedom's first.
I suppose in a way we lead and are led:
You feel the grapevine pulling at your tongue,
Then in among the clusters, buckshot sprayed.
What are arms for but halters and headstarts?—
Each man strains the tight circle of his friends.
I look at a love-ring on my finger
And know how much I am a swollen man.
The gold turns, a lavish island glimmers—
No wonder we love exotic language,
Dress our dreams only in fig leaves, and mime
And mime our rich incorporated power:
To keep in shape we stretch the skin of things.

Moonlight and Madness

It is the sort of thing you may have dreamt for years:
A man in the moonlight, lucid, cool, a little cruel,
As if the garden somewhere held a mammoth vase of tears.

Even in the dream you know it is a kind of craze—
These are the things discarded when you could not stand them
     anymore,
Drop by drop, too cold, too moonlit to be called the sweat of days.

For you have lain, as moist as any man, in her glorious arms,
Taken up the pen that scattered spots expanding like the sea,
And written of, not written off, a tale of her voluptuous charms.

Still, this sense of life's effluvia always underlies
The shotput in the sun, the stalled car, the pushing up the hill,
The strangely alabaster little tear running from her eyes.

This is when the promise of the moonstruck dream takes over.
No cup will do, no bowl—it must be something like a massive urn
To hold all we think that we have lost as athlete and as lover.

It never fills, it never tips—it is an icon on the moonlit land,
Almost comforting to those who struggled up the hill or kissed so
     much,
And felt bewildered muscles slacken, and the tear dry on the hand.

Hair of the Dog

Felled by a night stick or a coconut,
He woke and heard the chorus of the sea.
Was it in town or on the beach—that blow?
Would a cool mermaid bring him some nervine,
Or a rough from the town roll him again?
This is the nabob of the night before,
Always at home only among foreigners.
A necromancer of the non-ego,

He could look up and see his own comet
And say, ah, brilliance forever, the nerves
Still holding, holding, beaded with crystal.
He could expose his sex to the sun:
The night threads held and the plant did not die.
Was it too much Nesselrode and white wine,
Or did the boom fall, a head from the sky?
It is a curious moment, believe me,
When just enough becomes a bit too much:
A sudden tear puts a strain on the necklace;
An orange in hand sags like a bowling ball;
The landscape reels from alley to sea lane—
The world you commanded, a colander,
The juice of all judgment draining away.
Now, where, oh where, is passion's paraclete?
Among snapped cords, the nerves scatterd like beads,
The long livid scar on the burning scalp,
The enpurpled bruise on the upturned face,
One remembers the weight of the journey:
How the strange place flipped itself off and on
And you would guess, and guess wrong, where you were,
Your skin encoded with holes from the tin.
Listen, dear heart, this mixture of motives
And metaphors is meant merely to warn
The line, as it moves, against the sinker—
How else to bob the buoy in the heart?—
The sun will not take the hook from your mouth,
Your face in the wind like a punching bag.
Yes, I have had these mornings now and then,
The papaya eaten, the dropping rind,
Saved the woman from the plummet of her pearls.
I have seethed in fury at the heavy end,
Calming a little when the circles spread.
Offshore from sleazy bar and champagne glass,
You lick up the slack to that tight-coiled place
Where the first release is a diamond—
Made sleek, made handsome, and happy again,
You cannot refuse a hair of the dog.

III

Whistle Stop

Do you remember the jerkwater town,
The train with the cowcatcher coming through?—
The wish to see the throes of silk flanks,
The boredom buffered by tiger lilies
That lined the tracks, the paradox, mixture
Of motives, the sharp sense that a javelin
Thrown in your floral guts would make the world
Wince, that you waited and warded the blow?

Perhaps even the hammock where you lay
Under the cherry tree seemed a bit bagged
With explosive—questions in the blue sky,
The ripe fruit hung like red cedillas,
Across your face the scimitar of the sun,
The sudden cicatrice, the ropes next time—
An old-fashioned fan from Panama
Dividing the flies, the head plunging on.

The train passed by but left a pleonasm
In the town—flowers stuffing the iron throat
Of the tracks, long iced drinks in the gullet,
The fans laid low like huge abandoned moths,
A burning face sweating its *cire perdue,*
The crotch calling for the dark cabana—
Somehow it goes on tearing us apart;
The sound of the future is a whistle.

Perhaps most often in these towns it leaves
A much more swiped, swollen, hail, farewell:
The map of the skin rerouted with sweat,
The cabana invaded by the incubus,
A top hat in the closet stacked with smoke—
We wait—this time the train stops for water:
An aqueduct is running through the house—
The hand spreads, catching figments in the sun.

Folk Song

Having had your say, you can lie abed,
Dream of how the wind blows up the skirts of girls on lazy
    afternoons,
And lets the sailor in you plan a voyage and from their knees
    construe what Sirens said.

Having had your day—the afternoon is sunlit, long—
You do not need to stop at any port, or send a letter home.
As long as girls lift up their sails, the wind is strong.

It sings of purple passion, haze, and noon—
Get out your old guitar and strum on board
How folk like you live on, draw out the tune.

A little calm, and there are haystacks on the sea,
These skirts so full of seed and musk and sorcery,
And you must wait a while—but just a little while—their magic sets
    you free.

So you can say when you have played the field—
Only one, bright, billowed skirt, flapping in the wind,
And somewhere in the house a girl will murmur: Yield.

When you have had your day, it never fails—
You take an image that was always with you in the field:
The wind blows strong, the girls spread out their sails.

June Issue with Swan Dive

So this for us suggests the naked swan—
Under the feathers this lean, gold-washed man
Still lethal-eyed as if smothered too long,
His sunburned nose a touch of orange beak—
Confined in an Idea, you will come out
Looking for action, singed with energy,
Surprised to be ironically goose-bumped
As though the cool air plucked at pretension.
Still, the elation as the diver soars—
We are all packed with collapsibles.
I have seen lovers beaking each other,
Young men wrestling as if they gripped with wings,
The sibling yellow in a feathered bed.
We borrow the world wherever we wish—
The diver knows this, spreading his arms wide.
I could, of course, give you the malicious twist,
Let intensity burst white like a spray-can:
A foolish Christmas angel plummets down.
Sometimes it is better simply to take
The romantic appeal at face value.
The diver showering under a sunflower,
Washing his gold as the stretched skin flecks white,
Will pack up the bird in a tight, black suit—
I am one who is glad a swan allows
This instant exit from an interfold.

Cottonmouth

He came in from the wings in a time of drouth,
And shows me how one whose blood is heated by the sun
Turns to those who long for rain the implacable white mouth.

He knows where, under branches, there are hidden streams—
That venomous face shaped like a little pitcher spout
Could tell you, if it would, just how to pour your dreams.

For it is the time of pouring that you want, the coming down in
    sheets—
You, too, held in, held down, held back, too long
Would like to see emotion running down the streets.

You need a ceramist, you need to be a living jug
Set out in the sparsest rain to gather every meager drop:
What other passion could you borrow from the white mouth of
    that little thug?

So this is what you long for—your release—
What you have learned from the hot, never-ending summer.
Cut and run?—the path is blocked, across the way, to that coulisse.

It is strange how seldom weather compromises with the heart—
You want to pour with all the liquid of the world held back:
The cottonmouth is waiting in the wings to prompt the river if the
    storm should start.

Latchstring

Always this sense of forbidden places
Surrounds us as we give, take, go and turn—
It may be a garden filled with larkspur,
The name almost like a goad in the heart;
Or a view to the sea to the landlocked:
An aquamarine on a woman's hand,
A string of blue beads on a foam-white neck,
The room itself, a glazed aquarium.

Others turn that doorknob on the hill—
They want caves, grottos, and cold waterfalls,
The feeling that they hang gardens as they rise
And call the mountain lion to lick their fingers.
They may have spent long hours as children
Locked in closets for things they did not do.
It was indeed the mountain air coming in
When the key turned in the forgiving hand.

Have you not watched someone you really loved,
Lucidly loved, you thought, let down a veil

Of gauze and wait there in silent tableau
As if the curtain cords lacked some tension,
The finesse to lift, hitch up the vague film,
The doubt tucked up in the arch of the mind?—
It is a rare soul that is not cobwebbed
With these traces of inept performance.

No wonder we accumulate our keys
Like a fail-safe, desperate operation,
Rattle doors, read diaries, rape the strongbox,
Rage at the gates of *hortus conclusus*—
One more kiss may trip the lock where larkspur
Throb up around us in our throes of love—
We give, take, go, turn, the lick of the lion
Leads on—we lift the latchstring to the sea.

Regrets Only

Not so much the white phlox on the table
Nor the red wine glasses, though these released
The little drama of her elegance—
Nor the exquisite cakes, the green sherbet
Like the pale frozen rind of a melon—
That put us well within the woman's scope.
One came there knowing nothing, nothing at all:
She removed preconceptions at the door.
We were like lizards with a slow pulse of life,
Puffing in her face with our low-keyed fire.
She pulled us inside from backward history,
Gave us magical drinks in crystal cups
Lest the damp on our hides stain her satin chairs.
I have known such women, often blessed them,
Come in with the smile of a crocodile,
Having sunned too long in my own long-ago,
Glad of a morsel in a stunning dress,
Amazed the white rug did not show a drop of blood—
You are quite right to raise your doubts, demur
That women, rooms, like this can still exist.
We squirm, hide our green legs in trousers,

Stir from the plaza of primordial shape,
Knock on these doors with a horny hand
Only to be pulled out of our leather
By a wardrobe mistress changing costumes.
Some say she has indeed a marble hand
Which we come in from the sun to worship,
Something that coldly plucks us from ourselves—
But I eat the beautiful dishes like a prince.
Some of us forget to go home in our scales,
Some of us leave an armor on the lawn—
I regret how it must be for her, alone,
At night—that harsh sense of naked bodies,
The river rising with all its mouths open,
Her dreams spotted with colored oil as if she bit
Into her passion only when the rest were fed:
What if they ate her out of house and home?

Enigma of the Eye

Somewhere you may find it, your own deep shade,
Centered by a pool with waterfowl and flowers—
Somewhere you will eat the fruit, cool the blood, sheath the blade.

You will feel the everlasting breeze upon your face,
Sieve with groin and armpits the saturated, scented wind,
And know that you have come at last upon the secret watering
    place.

You must know and know and know the drouth,
How eyes, mouth, chest, sex go hot and tense—
You need to stand, as if it were an oriflamme, beside the myrtle of
    the South.

I know for I have held it up till almost evening and the flaming
    door,
Exhilarated and exaggerated by the absolutes of dust and fire,
With only the implacable desire to have this one lust more.

You hallucinate the trampled grass, the lion, rhinoceros,
And wonder if they have come before you, waded, wallowed,
Left the silver pool you counted on, pustulant and filled with pus.

This is what bubbles up, the waterhole without a drain—
Some cannot bear it when they find it in their own deep shade
As if an eye they silvered over glazed and would not clear again.

Roof Garden

How did we think of planting gardens on a roof,
The ornamental trees, the glittering fountain and the flowerbeds,
As though of our ascent from some superior somewhere we gave
    living proof.

Is it that it sank too deep and low, our Eden lost,
And once we brought it to the surface of the ground
We kept on lifting, lifting it at any cost?

The Grand Hotel, its management and staff, both suave, astute,
Have every inch soigné, brilliant in the sun, glamorous at night,
Gardeners from the basement up, expert at stretching root.

This is the garden you and I have dreamed of, lover—
At noon, the pink marquee, the blush and rush of blood,
And something smooth and silver in our drinks when the day is
    over.

There is nothing in the world like making love aloft.
The fountain in the wind, our bodies sway and curve,
Some blossoms fall, and dancing cheek to cheek is petal-soft.

We fell from grace—the mighty, fallen, make it right.
The silver drink, the petaled cheek, the ecstasy of lengthened
    root—
Is it only fantasy, or do we keep on rising through the night?

IV

The Gangplank

Even the soft pink grape of the palate,
A loose eyelash wandering in the eye
Might be just too much and tip you over.
Could it be the weight of light on the skin,
Or your suntan hiding deep resources?—
Climbing the ladder you seemed to gain weight:
Then that sudden lurch to the right, and down,
A loud scream like jettisoned ballast?

One needs a certain calm flatness of tone
To tell of mounting doubts, acquisitions
Like phlegm swallowed on the tongue—not the rich
Indigestible meal, ostentatious ring,
But accumulations of stale sweat
Which come up, a kind of human ozone,
When you reach the end of the diving board—
These are the killers in the comedy.

You know you do not really want to dive—
On out, out, a brilliant sea to walk on.
Let them have the pink pendant in your throat,
Let them frisk you of all your pendulous past.
I have seen men stand there preening, sun-mad,
Rubbing down their worst compulsions with oil.
Try it someday, as if basic body,
Pushed at last, barters for the basic soul.

48

Sword of Damocles

If someone replaced the hair with nylon,
You may be safe for a while, but do not
Count upon it—that still, glittering point
Wants to split the brain, down to the duramen
As if the fearful heart had turned to wood—
You have stood under the elevated
Railroad and waited for it to fall, you
Have borne the waterfall's drop hammer
And given your shoulders as architrave,
But this sword is quite another matter—
Like an extracted tongue, perhaps your own,
It longs for the amorous body lost,
Gleaming and gleaming with its silver lust,
Hung there to remind us that we may be
Forever divided by what we say.
Speak the wrong word, the lingual stretch,
And you have a lover split to the groin.
Stand there instead under your own sharp talk
And you yield like a melon to metal.
Sometimes the sword hangs down, soft, silkily,
Like a rope pull to open heaven's door,
As if wanting to be struck like a chime.
But touched without tact, the electric needle
Leaps to the skin, flowing manic pictures—
All those dancers, all the slim, glowing youth
Know the dagger hides in the chandelier.
The lissome leg slides from the slit ball gown,
A moustache looks silvered with the blade's sweat—
I come out of all this dreaming trauma
With a small, wavering point of knowledge,
The grasped compass come down from the gallows,
As if the hung weight drifts on with the tribe.
Sense it in the street as the light changes,
That moment when you were stalled and not stabbed,
The café, the lover waiting unriven—
Still held in an awning the words to come.

The Blue Train

There he was, going down the coast—the *wagonlit*—
The Blue Train overnight, holding the pale, white man
Who wanted to lie like a sponge at the bottom of the sea.

He tried a drink, read a novel, but the page
Leaked off into the night somewhere, a blue miasma,
And nothing in that hurtling, tight compartment could assuage.

You see, some of us are born to want ineffable blue drink,
To soak it up in every etiolated pore—
Wherever oceans are, we would be the sink.

Morning comes—groggy and a little sick,
We wonder if oranges hang like tiny buoys by the sea,
Pushing back the blue moons on our nails with—what else?—an
    orange stick.

Because you see we do not want to be quite lost—
We mean to come up from the depths, wear the blue mantle in the
    sun,
Swing the oranges like censers for our Pentecost.

Still, you may ride all night and never take the plunge—
Just the sun's ocellus on the hand in the dining car:
The spot of peacock blue—no more than this one squeezes from
    the sponge.

Flaws

If one could choose them, it might go better:
A lip-sore from the petal of a rose,
A blue pox shaken from the hydrangeas,
The gold squama on the naked swimmer
Standing in the blue frame of a peerless day—
If they were not something that we must hide:
The absurdity of the safety pin

That holds the elegant outfit together,
The hole in the sock just below the heel
Of the shoe, the slip, in prolapse, hitched up.
Even the violet scent from the French bath
Cannot lose our aura to the bloodhounds—
Is it any wonder the mottled hand
Comes forward with its rich, jeweled finger
To cow, humiliate those liver spots,
The blue chiffon dress like smoke in the eyes,
Wavering, billowing where flesh would bulge,
Or the old dandy curries his top hat,
The bald spot calling for help like a leper?
We redirect the traffic when we can—
The eyeshadow that lets down and lifts a shade
On eyes too filled with sunrise and sunset:
Who knows what time, what hour, the soul desires?
A Malacca cane—who says you stagger/
A head in diamond halter wins by a neck—
Still we keep on counting on that clear morning,
That evening, indeed that bright sun at noon,
When we will be so filtered of our flaws—
While this other slightly freighted figure
Balances and mends an unrigged world:
The petal on the lip, blue confetti
On the shoulders, the showering swimmer
Shaking water like sequins from his skin.

Bitter Pill

Some try to coat it with views of the sea,
This secret pellet in the heart of life.
Others glance at the sun, then look away,
The point of vision quickly gold-plated.
A few, knowing we are made of water,
Inland drawn, trill a dewdrop on their tongues.
The upthrust nipple of the lover charms
The lips—can love be swallowed bit by bit?

There are bluepoint oysters and fine champagne
That softly line the palate, heat the blood
With these ambiguities of instructions—
Can we syncopate our swoon of longings?
Straight whisky has a blunter thing to say:
Why not build a small bonfire in the gut—
It can burn for hours, and then who cares
If the bed is a grate of dead embers?

She might give you a bead from a necklace
Broken when you claimed far too much, too fast,
A pacifier to roll in the mouth
When the rage for rich absorption returns.
But it melts, almost metaphysically,
As you dream and dream of the bitter end.
The lozenge, blue or gold, you meant to take?—
The lake below the tongue cannot recall.

Snapback

Perhaps it was the hibiscus by the pool
Or perhaps the hate letter in the mail,
The red horn flaring on the dark green plant,
The enclosed packet of cantharides:
You are not the man you thought you were,
You are not the last of the red hot poppas,
Someone snorkeling there in the blue sea
Is watching you, a one-man submarine.
Which one of your lovers sent Spanish fly
To suggest that your sex life needs sparklers,
Some light in the cave of concupiscence?
Just the effort of putting a stickpin
In your shirt makes the mat of the heart wince.
That dripping figure in the rubber suit
Is coming ashore to spear you in the groin,
The soldier of fortune she really loves.
It will not do to endure strappado,
Setting up the silk ropes in your own room,
If cushions are piled as high as your soles—

It begins much more modestly than this,
Picking the swimmer's image from the eye,
These squamae of inversion, these flakes of sight—
Taking the hibiscus by the warm throat
And telling it that you can name that tune,
Blushing gold in the mirror from the black suit,
Giving the opal in the pin your chest
For a fire dance—I know there will be throes,
The offshore threatening and the in-house slough,
But there is a bright beetle you can grind,
Tongue-kissing the letter you send her.
You can make the dropped silk ropes rise and dance
To the music throttled from that lush flower.
There is always a window in the cave,
Eye of the bull that first saw red. You sluice
The wet suit with a wounded hero's blood,
Unwind tangled nerves from their cat's cradle—
The pulled rapture lands you like a lizard in the sun.

The Bit

It seemed he was slipping away from himself—
Too much headlong love, too much food and wine,
Her pearls on the bureau flung like a curb,
His brown belt on the floor like a dropped cinch.

The impetuous had been so beautiful—
One more kiss, one more glass of wine, a surge
That could not be held back or brought up short—
Her crystal earrings tinkled as they danced

Like the chandelier on a fast night train.
Every jolt felt the buffer of her breasts,
Only that horse pawing in the boxcar,
Only that scent of the flanks on her skin.

Was it the moment she drew down the shades
As though putting those blinders on the world

They felt some leeway in the sensual stretch?—
Always, always, there was one more length.

Then, as if all the way back to the end,
One could feel the compartments linked and linked,
As though one finally felt the hold-up,
The rude, masked bandit collecting his loot.

You drop your rings, my studs like lost nails
From a horseshoe, flecks of foam on my lips
As I chafe at the sudden, snapped-back force,
The fantasy with metal in its mouth.

If we wake to blood in the throat next day,
It may be in fact just the tongue bitten,
It may be in truth just the taste of gall—
A rinse of the real is all we need.

But, nevertheless, the rash, brash mixture—
Sometimes the urge is irresistible
To fall back into each other's arms
To the sound of the sliding boxcar doors.

Out there, free and swallowing blood for us,
The horse has taken the bit in his teeth—
You lift up a lid of the tight-drawn shades:
One eye is enough for a world full tilt.

In Vino Veritas

Loneliness was all around him like a purple light—
It was late August and the grape-colored dahlias hung heavy:
Nothing in the private or the public world seemed right.

It was not that people did not visit, come to dine,
But that they came, heavy as dahlias with boredom and sorrow,
And when they left, the sky was deeper-tinged like wine.

How did it come about? Why this instead of that?—
He is an immaculate man, born life-giving, life-loving,
Not a sign upon his socks that he is prone to trampling in the vat.

Somewhat weary of the world, and yet no waster,
Committed to a clear regard for vintage, premier cru,
He has become of violet light impeccably the taster.

Someone will bring him now and then a bottle of rosé,
Tinted with roses of Anjou, tinged with tourmaline,
A delightful ordinary wine without a single extraordinary thing to
    say.

A cellar for the rare occasion?—Even the dahlias know its must—
But there is something in these white-socked, suited men, unloved,
    perhaps unlovable,
Who pour into the world with steady hand a light that I can trust.

The Pump

So now his pomegranate days were over,
Only swallowed pulp, seeds in his teeth,
The engulfment of the sea's dazzling sequins,
The sun's long, deep burn and the moon's lip salve,
The night wine going down cool like silver,
The fantasy that the skin will expose
Us, coming back with splotch and purpura.
I do indeed feel this hidden leaching:
The sun bringing up a pimple of its fire,
The much-kissed lips sagging with their stencil,
The rolled-over body, kneaded, rising,
The popgun effect of our sentences
As if the mouth were loaded with word-shot—
We do not measure, do not mean to miss
A single source that any season gives:
Hothouse peaches in winter and rich cream,
The enclosed verandah glazing the sea,
The sunlamp's power of poaching, chest and thigh—
It seems, therefore, a bit too much to ask

That we can be rinsed of so much rapture:
The cosseting sun, the cosmetic moon,
The sea taking back its rich, bright spangles,
The phantoms fading down in the wine's weir,
A lover pulling off the old bruises.
But you and I work double time on this,
Listening somewhat better for each other,
Your head at my heart, my lips at your breast,
This bringing up the very deepest brim
As if the sound of the soul were a pump—
I do not know what fountain we expect,
But on our very fairest days we flush
As if we mingled rainbows in our depths.

Night Cap

The man decided that it was a day to do as you please—
Why not pull a voluptuous blue ocean up to a beach chair?
Why not feel the siren sitting on his knees?

So many cautious, cancelled days of ifs, don'ts, buts—
The tall, lean psyche longs to scale the palm tree,
Instead of tears, drop down upon the head of negatives delicious
    coconuts.

A slash of the knife, the straw put in the milk—
We have spent years contemplating hemlock:
The time has come for Socrates to think of sipping silk.

It will do wonders for an irritated lining,
This drink from the green cup one shares with a figment on the
    knee—
No accusations of perverted youth or serious social undermining.

Ah, that blue, that green, that strange, romantic face!—
What is the couch and all the puzzled pupils gathered round
Compared with rich symposia—the gold, the sunset cloth, the
    banquet place?

One asks, but then the pinch—the most seductive day is over.
Twitch the blue, thump the tree—athlete of aftertaste—
Direct the moon to put some silver in the hemlock of the lover.

V

The Concert Grand

It looks lonely there untouched by any human hand,
A wing grown stolid now that it has been stalled,
Chockablock, as if it made its way from some far Cubist land.

The poet may get this feeling, having written but not struck home:
No one to memorize his lines, no vocal chords to quiver—
Just this stillness of a wilderness in which he chose to roam.

The instrument, magnificent, meant to sing, to sigh, to roar—
It has been used and used and used, but now this desuetude:
No one is sitting in the audience, no one is coming in the door.

Still, I am here, and run my fingers on the unused keys—
It seems a flight of doves has broken from the brilliant mouth
As if to bless the fact that I sit down, make music as I please.

Pax vobiscum. Project! Project! The birds light in the rows.
The crowds are coming in from here, there, from Cubist land—
How many you can hold in thrall at last God only knows.

The wild, the tender strain, the simple passage, and the one of
    guile—
I stand, look into the dark, the strings like pulsing vocal chords:
The poet, a long-lost brother, is coming down the aisle.

The Cane

I do not mean to tell the cabala
Of the cane, but merely that I saw it
In the hall beside the pale yellow gloves
In the sunlight. Things choose me this way, glow,
Gloat even for their text and exegesis.
I know then that I am truly alive:
The light comes from a laser from within,
And I must pounce upon the walking stick.

The subject then is these clear connections—
Pick up the cane, put on the yellow gloves,
A ghost no longer wanders in the mind.
Morning's attitudes come in to clothe you,
The clean shirt, the good suit, the pearl-gray hat.
You have been invaded at close quarters—
That voodoo in the sun, that cane, those gloves:
One wonders what the spirit did all night.

Now one can shuffle leaves, poke chanterelles
That smell like the plum of coming summer,
They, too, with their yellow chosen by the sun.
And now one is a chip off the old block,
The first man incited by images, made
Solid on this elegant morning—
It always takes some doing to fatten
The wraith found loitering in the mirror.

So it can be a spectral place, this world,
Or one where Jazzbo Jim picks up the cane
And lays about in his brilliant tap dance,
The bright synapses snapping everywhere.
Keep hankering for that sparkle in the hall:
It is enough for a life to have learned
How incurably physical we are,
And how incorrigibly of the mind.

Stylebook

Take, with some authority, a blue sea,
Take dawn, sunset, according to your mood.
Take a woman—Optional: nude or dressed,
On the beach itself or overlooking it.
All of this presupposes a mindset:
This is no tearjerker, no book of sighs—
You mean to make an example, instruct
Yourself in how another day is lived.

The sea itself will evade perfection,
Rumpled and corpulent, belching with foam.
The blood-veins in the sky look varicose;
The woman is not quite state of the art,
And now your point of view seems dubious.
You should never be so close as the beach,
The balcony where you stand looks too vapid:
Just models, no central intelligence.

Nevertheless, these choices cling and cling—
Winter, now, and some wet snow on the shoes.
You are a barbarian wandering in dread,
The skins and the thongs cannot keep out the cold.
Did that confident day happen elsewhere?—
You still have a stiff finger in the book,
Groin of a picture wincing at your touch.

Postscript for Locke

The poet had written so much, so much, so much,
Far back as tabula rasa where the first stylus moved—
Every piece of paper in the world had felt his touch.

In desk and closet, under the bed in old suitcases full of
    manuscript—
The evolutionary style, now a legend in its time, moved on
And so did the futuristic roller of pulp, endlessly equipped.

59

Much more static, outside the window, his own beckoning blue
     spring
Paused, posed, like the one gorgeous, ineffable peacock
Which cawed and cawed in the scratching pen and could not be
     made to sing.

And there, just a little further on from where he sat,
Like Tom Thumb who never got a franchise in his life,
The topaz blisters in the golf course were soothed and soothed to
     emerald matte.

He closed the window, pulled the shades down to no avail:
There was a shimmering green glow along the wall,
The spots before his eyes were taken from the peacock's tail.

Is this then one of long, long writing's basic laws?—
The blue spring gets into the ink, emeralds come down from the
     wall and seep across the floor,
The lyric lingers, lingers on the page, the peacock caws.

The Folly

Summer was almost over—it was time
To condense his sensations. He went down
To the folly with a book, a platter
Of fruit, like Faunus, tamed, self-committed.

How golden-haired and woolly he had grown
These months, ticked all over with this brilliance.
Fondling, fondled like melons in the field,
His mouth always smeared with berries.

If they plugged him in at the big house
To tingle their nerves as they touched, stroked him,
Shifting weight he could sway the chandeliers—
His shoes left peach juice on the spotless rug.

So wet and yet so full of wire, he might
Have shocked himself in contact with her lips;

He smiled, withdrew, and shut down the current,
Zipping up the tight fruit-suit as he left.

The green copper dome, the Grecian columns,
A bench overlooking a white lake—
It was like an open bell for all his glut;
Even his heart could hang there like a watch.

She might have left behind her scented scarf,
A collapsed snake lying in the corner.
The book flapped, the loose fruit rolled from the plate,
Suspenders snapped with the burden of sex.

How could he make the folly seem less foolish?—
Screened by the trees, he could strip naked, do
His exercises with the large dumbbells,
Turning, whirring like his inner works.

But even they glossed up quickly, paused
Like balls hanging from a pawn shop,
The heart a little too gilt from its hook,
His fallen shorts shackles in the sunlight.

So another day wanted his fingerprints:
Lines filled with the perfumed fat of women,
A topography of the taken fruit—
The ink of his lavish intimacy.

How do we justify these one-man ghettos?—
One sits, sweat drops from the bench like globules
Of the lush and shatterproof alembic,
The self unaltered like a drip-dry shirt.

Still, there is a lucid, charged impression,
Autumn and its beautiful solitaire—
A lead urn receives our fallen leaves;
A face, a figure, look tooled all over.

In the big house the white curtains flutter
But no one yet has given up the ghost,
And Faunus reads his hand like a palmist,
The lifeline deeper than it was before.

Squeegee

When he went up and down the window pane,
There was a picture on the other side
Of a young man he thought he used to be:
Clear, stark, bold, a blue pool, a tan swimmer,
An hibiscus flaring in a corner.
It was like peeling back an outer layer,
The scum of time leached from a bleary eye—
It had the true depth of the heart in it.

Sometimes, more passively, we sit in a car
And the windshield wiper will scrape the world:
Just a bit of it, a wedge, a folding fan,
And a sense of clarity escalates—
The lovely, hyperkinetic snapshot,
A dazzling tree, a girl hitching a ride,
Soaked through with every tear the eye held back—
Next, the waterfall pouring through the car.

Somewhere, no doubt, a fat slush fund for those
Who have wrung out, wiped off, the scene for good—
But I keep on clearing, cleaning, where I can:
Half-moons on splattered windshields as they dry,
The shades drawn down on the voyeur's rapt eye.
Still, an album, free of sludge, accummulates:
The dripping swimmer, and the tear-soaked girl—
The lullaby of looking, page by page.

The Glass Head

It was suggested as a bit of a joke
That the confused man should sip silica,
Clearing the cloudy agate of his brain,
This white mineral honey through all his thoughts,
Coating a complex until its surface
At least appeared to be bland, translucent:
All that woolgathering turned to warp and woof,

If nothing more lucid, a tapestry—
The Unicorn and the Virgin perhaps—
But this is not the desired objective.
The psychiatrist would prefer his head
To be a spool from which he could pull out
The spider thread, the skating arachnid
A necessary evil on a tensile web
Which held the clear dewdrops of disclosure.
But the poor man, bless him, was a Gothic type
Who liked arches and groins and rose windows
And always spelled nave as if it were *knave,*
An avenue for the rogue, the oddball,
The *lusus naturae*—the labyrinth's throat
Which led into less than Amazing Grace.
One day he bit his doctor just to prove
Apostles of light are powered by blood.
Should any of us be too hard on him?—
Let those who can throw a headlight do so,
Or emulate a fishbowl when they talk,
Circular with gold and satisfaction.
Some of us shudder, too shy for glass heads—
The hawk that hides in the cathedral preens
His feathers, pink and blue, by the window,
The falconer, below, with cabin fever—
Will the world drunk through a filter give us
The lyrebird singing in a crystal tree?

VI

End Game

Go into these rich rooms again, the old familiar haunts,
The elaborate screens, birds, flowers, the woman standing:
Something for every sense and mood—all that the body wants.

Still, you hesitate, remembering that Goethe said
The threshold is always the place to pause—
What if the screens are folded, birds decapitated, the flowers and
  the woman dead?

In the life of the senses lurks the notion of an ultimate sin—
Having known too many endings, you never want them to
  conclude,
And, quite simply, the trick of all tricks may be: Never begin.

Dear lover—and it is a dark and musky act of love—
You do, and do not, wish to go into the room, your hand on the
  doorknob:
It would be like a violent act of sex if someone gave a shove.

Naked once again to screens, birds, flowers, perhaps an
  impassioned hand—
All the old hungers, ecstasies, accumulate outside the door,
But there is something new in this you do not understand.

You want to enter without tremor, but you do not want to blend—
For once, why can't the assembled world decide, without your
  presence,
How we can knit a long beginning to a very little end?

Jacaranda

I have too much trouble, studying my dreams:
That jacaranda tree, that lovely girl,
The purple bandeau around her dark hair—
It is as though the deep lines in the palm,
Dry though they seem, could still run off somewhere,
That one goes on deltaing forever.
So I give my hand to another girl—
Her blue eyes mist to violet, the tree
Hangs in a purple flag near the river.
I close my hand like a vise to grasp
Two moments together, the closed waterways,
Backed up, pulsing, sucking on amethyst—
But she spreads out my hand again—the stone
Has left an imprint of those lips—fingers relaxed,
The tree shakes down its blossoms there—
I could feel the color flow from my hand
As though from a fatal birthmark on the heart,
Rich, so it seemed, on from the table's edge.
Not even the old, fat, ominous gipsy
Wearing fake amethyst in a fillet
Could ever make the hand look fully drained
As if a kiss rose from the headwaters
Where all the commercials have their source.
I change to another station, the girl
Enlarged, hangs lifeless pigmies from her wrists.
I sit, sunk in my chair's collapsed canoe—
What other gesture than the hand outspread
Comes and goes in a purple surf of dreams?

Belvedere

It is not Apollo that you really wish to see in the belvedere,
But your own sleek, sloughed-off, most enigmatic self
As if the old lifeline enjambed, and in the basic nude you were
    standing there.

65

Yes, there is another sentence, and, so you think, it speaks the
     truth—
Those gleaming muscles, tendons, propelled by inner drive,
Select from their allotment this shining figure of a youth.

Up high, up there, because the secret mind adores high art—
You look down on the dump and all the rubber tires,
Call in the truck for just one more, and tell it to depart.

It is a funny thing, this taking something that belongs in Rome,
And on this balcony reenacting something like its pose
Just because you believe it never really found a final home.

The engram must have stuck, a picture in your high school days,
And in this handsome, hidden enclave on a hill,
You can unwrap the figure for its final phase.

The view is still there—alas, the smouldering and the rubber
     tires—
What would we do if all the pictures, statues, of the world
Could not travel even for a day as far as our desires?

Dumbbells

It seemed an impossible blue current,
With far-off banks and the body weighted,
Even the birds offering their sharp beaks
Like electric needles for swift tattoo,
The flesh coded and stamped against abduction—
All this as you were using the dumbbells,
Stripped naked and brilliant in the sunlight.
When they were locked to your wrists, the shackles
Clamped on tight, you knew that it meant business.
Someone was selling you down the river,
The slave burned blue, the exotic plantation,
The mind, too, perceived as its own dead weight—
No paddle wheels, no pink Mississippi
For you, the water flamingo-colored,
The radiant dawn, umbrellas waiting.

Somehow that day as you lifted your arms
With their weights, you flashed this picture and held
It a moment above the waterline—
They could see your nerves stretched,
Espaliered, like a net for their haul
And swag—At this point it is time to consider
Just what you were lifting in the sunlight,
How the smooth calves were lichened with leg irons
And someone bundled you off on the barge.
Is this what sometimes happens just to those
Who are somewhat overtrained for happiness?—
Not keeping the dumbbells light as sucked eggs,
Leaving the skin slightly oiled for escape—
Learning to thread that rich river through an eyelet
To be pulled taut by the point of your life.
Dear Lord, how these private gymnasiums
Spawn the indigo slaves down the delta,
Their spent lungs still pinked with passion—
Advised, some use a mirror for practice,
Pause when the blue sweat races the river.
Some, but just some few, have pawned their dumbbells
To keep astute Adonis out of hock.

The Ablution

The man considered his options: nothing in the mind and, most
    certainly, nothing visible out there.
Years before ecstasy had come sliding down to him on a shaft of
    light;
All that he had to do was think a little, just a little, and then stare.

Somewhere a predatory eagle had released a smiling cherub,
An alter ego sitting in a gleaming pool of light,
Who followed him, after cigarettes and coffee, into his morning
    tub.

Consider how this naked man bathed the amorino, putto,
Gave no thought to how the eagle's wicked eye, somewhere above,
Was letting him, for just a little while, put on his show.

How did it happen—first light, then dark, then empty space?
You have seen these well-scrubbed, well-dressed men along the
    street
With something like an eagle's scratches on their face.

There must have been a moment though, not ever seen,
When these extremes that somehow loved each other
Nestled and caressed—one to be held and one to preen.

What did they whisper, tell each other, what confide?
Some harmony of strength and charm, a tale of the tub?—
The spout that pauses, starts, stops, like children coming down a
    slide.

Sunflower Souvenir

The aging swimmer—do you remember him?—
Young, tan, bright as a sunflower,
Taking the light, almost stolidly, hour by hour,
As if nothing in his world ever could go dim.

The brilliant sunflowers are still there,
Tall, eternal, a symbol of his life—
What was it then which used the knife
On him so that sunlight seems to leave a tear?

A tear, a rip, a wound across the day,
A latent, livid scar along his face—
The machete working in the fields of grace
Seems to bring the swimmer down upon his knees to stay.

This is what comes of flower-measure—
Rest and bloom, rest and bloom—
Cut and in a vase, a sunflower in a room,
Cyclically secure, can be a heavy thing of pleasure.

But swimmers have no benefit of pollen—
The voluptuous sweat must take the hint

And leave beside the pool a shadow-print,
The sense of something of a life forever fallen.

We see him rise, the swimmer down upon his knees,
Just before the heavy flowers talk,
Just before the long knife hits the stalk,
As if he saved forever some portion of the ways we please.

The Plane

Do not mind if the golden curls come up
Around the hand as if you were shaving
A lover's head found to be prostitute.
If you are deflected by an image
So amorous, you will seldom succeed,
The world full of gold hair regretted,
A seizure of tears smelling of sawdust.
Unless the love of the wood keeps calling,
You will never learn the use of the plane.
When the first thick shavings fall to the floor,
Medusa will be knocking at your ear,
And, on demand, you will give her the snakes.
Rather make your back, like Perseus, a shield
Reflecting that which might never exist.
It can be motion orgasmic as sex,
Not knowing when you will stop till you stop,
The released stroke, instinctive quietus,
The assuaged concern, and the perfect fit.
So we go daily somewhat into depth:
A word used, shaved of its misconceptions,
The eye grown shrewd in its focus—no small
Thing when you think how it sluices itself.
Not that you wish to be given a plane
For Christmas, not that you want all Sundays,
Back and forth, so that the retracted scull
Can never seduce the rich blue river,
The punter rest among water lilies
As the world blurs into rapt blissfulness
And the lover, recovered, is thick with hair.

One speaks an anxiety of attitudes,
As though a weighted blade moves across the brain
And the one curl too much will hiss and strike—
A slither of river, a lurching boat—
The hand upon the pole is never sure
Whether to push on or pause in bogs of gold.

The Junk

One counts on it—a certain part of life is irremediably sunk,
Over, done with, and often for the best, down at the bottom of the
    sea,
When some sunrise, sunset, it surfaces, bizarre, outré, a Chinese
    junk.

What does this say to us about our inner sea?—
Things put down in haste, horror, even love, wanting still to float,
Disjecta membra, rising in a special pleading that they were meant
    to be.

It may not be the woman after all but still a woman, and her eyes,
Near dawn, turning toward you, make you wish that this were all.
But what is that disturbing and exotic shape upon the sea at
    sunrise?

Nothing more, perhaps, than what the very best of us repress:
Something held back by her, by you, indeed the world at large—
When and where it went down into the depths is anybody's guess.

The urge is always: roll over—back to sleep—
The day must be lived with glimpses of breaking green canoes,
    gondolas, stranger craft:
You cannot keep a large repressive hand, here, there, everywhere
    upon the deep.

The sunset smokes and smokes as though in flames to end the
    tale—
On the terrace with your best beloved in your arms,
You kiss and try to turn her back to something florid under sail.

Last Straw

It could well be as small as a needle
Or loom like a lighthouse on the landscape—
But a needle no less that lusts tattoo,
Blue pictures that bleed, wilful of inlay,
The lighthouse that picks your sense of grandeur
As if you gave it the sky to appliqué.
One may start out modestly each morning:
Devour a gentle poem with your orange juice,
Put a finger on a lover's soft lip
As if an arm or a hug were too much—
Start, as you will, the study of finesse,
Working from bread, perhaps, to ladyfingers,
The cream in the bowl with red raspberries,
A tension turning the water to wine,
Until the kiss sets a ruby on her lips.
There must be some of this, something of that—
Even the sun warns of its livid scar
When you stay by the cracked blind much too long,
The voyeur abstained from the virile voyage.
Nevertheless, that swimmer at summer's end
May feel like an ingot on the water,
Find that water lilies burn like gas rings,
A deadweight or the fluid, smelted gold—
One way or the other, waste on its way,
While the man behind the blind taps out
His cigarette before the bright haystack
In the field goes up in flames. I will not
Advise you whether a plum too much will
Stop your breath, a gold pen precariously taken
May kill a love letter, for I can see
A suttee of limbs near the haystack, smell
The gas flare in the lilies, feel the dross
Of an ingot on my thighs. Whether it
Began with the collapse of the thing withdrawn
Or a finger laid on a wincing lip,
Maunder of needles, might of the lighthouse,
I pick a straw as if it sipped my life.

Asbestos Book

He had climbed it so often, and now the top was red,
That palm tree heavy with nuts, so languorously, luxuriously
    coifed—
Was the sun at last, in fact the sunset in his head?

Had the blue sky gone home for good, not wanting to be
    scorched?—
He sat upon the summit of something, no doubt about it,
His bronze skin, moist and oiled from his ascension, waiting to be
    torched.

This can happen in the greenest and most blessed isles—
You have explored the crystalline streams, your teeth rotten from
    sweet fruit,
Experimented ad infinitum with all the nude and native styles.

That is when, toward evening, you will go in search
Of that last emerald tree you had sequestered there:
Nothing in the lucid day suggested any overflorid perch.

It looks now simply overlooked, that startling image—
The delicious wind turned the pages of your island log,
And here and there you must have skipped a high, unblemished
    page.

So naked, brown, and burnable—do not, do not, burn the book—
It is the perfect place way up in the flaming air
To roast a little, read a little, from the rubric of those pages stuck.

Life Preserver

At just this juncture, the life preserver
Floated by, a huge eye with blue iris—
The obsessive sea looked at me again.
It blinked back and forth in the waves, and I
Was hypnotized by this large ocellus.

My own eyes shimmered with peacocks, gold nudes,
Some old, luxuriant mixture of life,
An almost delirious visual dance.
I was being given an eye signal,
A blessing to bear up and to prevail,
To let the submerged sympathies arise,
A man on the beach, a peacock halo,
To blink, blink again, with the blinkable,
To let the passing detritus look in.
It was indeed an old, worn, white rim
With this voluptuous, roving center,
Too late perhaps for someone on a ship,
A lost, imbedded sorrow of the sea.
It could have gone past me, blue-inflamed,
The too swiftly turned, wall-eyed look of chance.
I have pondered and pondered these subtleties,
How one day we respond, another not,
How a prism in the pulsing hand darts
And darts, a collapsed bird, an uncrushed eye,
How the world swims and swims with assistance:
One day you grasp it, and another not—
When the life preserver sank out of sight,
The gold man with the halo round his head
Reviewed a long festival of feeling:
The day was clear and calm as lucite,
The pupil and the passion filled with light.

The Country of the Blue (1994)

I

Cahoon's Hollow, Looking Down

Melville admired a whale because he went five miles downstairs,
Perhaps, beneath that pressure, feeling more alive—
Man, perforce, must make a much more shallow dive:
Beautiful swimmer with his lodestone of despairs.

But, summer of the sea, you do not need discount the grace
Of swimmers, nor against their courage cavil,
When they must circumscribe and kiss the navel
Of the water in some blue, impassioned, minuscule embrace.

Forget the metaphor, forget the whale, remember when,
Smelling of salt, perhaps indeed remiss,
The swimmer must unfinger the seductive kiss,
Spread out, like joined antitheses, his dual, two-vaned fan.

While heart hammers secret, battered images against the ground,
It seems, great plunger, you incited him
To such dissatisfaction with his natural rhythm
That he looks fallen there from stairs whose final step he found.

The Javelin

After what seemed a cosmic orgasm,
The shuddering sky, the frenzied birds,
He woke up by the atoll's blue lagoon
As if pinned there like an afterimage,
Something not supposed to go in the glow—
The flamingos had flown, the sky was calm,
But something like a javelin held him
In place, stuck with this strange everafter.

One eye opened, a fanlight on the world:
A very ordinary man subdued,
The warm print of a woman by his side—
Two eyes, and his whole destiny came back:
This morning feeling of being impaled,
Trussed, in bed, though he was fully naked.
Something, someone, wanted his heart left there,
And so it was, like the only keepsake.

Sometimes the imprint will cost just this much,
The imagination so overspent,
The woman, birds, hiding on the island,
And just this rich compensatory scene
As if one were at least well laid out for love—
I suspect you know these mornings after,
The absurd dreams with the main point plunged in:
One always lives in a hail of happenstance.

I put it to you now much more simply—
Even the swizzle stick in the strong drink
Lends its lissome weight, stalls on an ice cube.
Her dropped earring has a light lethal point,
The lore of the whetstone in manic birds—
But you will learn to move each day, transfixed,
While the javelin wavers in the air
As if it still knows the qualms of winning.

Palmy Days

Even the lover left in the lurch spreads
His hand like a frond, wanting and asking.
Stranded on the island with that rich palm,
He remembers the feel of her ripe breasts.

Now is the time to make a brilliant life
Of being underestimated, judged
As a castoff from the sensuous sea,
A man dumped back on his own desire.

What does one do in this situation?—
Go back to the six, seven, fantasies
A day?—the one gloriously fulfilled:
The coming in together on surf boards,

The huge white horn of a curling wave,
The sprawled plenty on the beach, lip and breast,
Under the very tree you now implore,
This idol with sealed fountain at the top.

It is time to be theatrical, trash
The bloodstream with extreme pictures, milk oil,
Palm-sugar from the tree, and remember
How your bodies were like a pair of tongs

That could pick up compressed desire, squander
It in cubes, one lump, or two, through the long
Afterswoon of love, the diminished thump,
The sea combing through a finished thing.

I will not leave a mist of metaphors,
The foghorn moaning, calling to failure—
That clear day is a diamond in the brain.
We lay on its table, hiding facets.

The undersides of what we would not see,
This keeping troubles to ourselves, this lie
Of riches, that the sea was not too bland,
That no hammer could split the perfect stone.

Still, by the tree, among brilliant splinters,
I must be the pointillist with the paste
And you the undine of the underside:
Here is the taste of your soul from my lips.

On this mosaic of broken diamonds,
It is so hot it burns our tender feet—
I have some little shade in my spread hand:
The slashing tree spikes sunlight everywhere.

Blue Landscape

In that blue landscape the sky is full of rooks:
The saturated blue and those excited cries—
You will not find the likes of this in ordinary books.

The color seems to blow like smoke, the lead bird swerves—
If I were dressed in denim, a life of Riley sort of man,
I would not like to come upon the secret of my nerves.

This is certainly not the place for luscious life, love, mating—
The full-blown has been altogether swept away,
And on its stem we feel the brain quietly pulsating.

The rooks are casing crops from their perch on hay:
You must be a sorry and sardonic sight to them,
Having wandered here from absinthe and the blue café.

It is exactly just the time to hoot and clap your hands:
I am Apollo rising in the sunlight with ambrosial locks
And not the latest member of earth's lost tribes and wandering
    bands.

This is an exercise—practice it on Riley's time, the luxe, the
    luscious living—
The world is mediocre, limp, without something like this force,
A god in this blue field to rout the rooks of your misgiving.

80

Long Hours in the Sun

Do you remember, all those years ago, long hours in the sun,
To the beach, and back again, always moving free of shadow?—
Few words were even thought, and spoken—for long hours—not
    one.

You did not think a single minute on how life aborts—
The fruit was ripening, the sea was full, the trees were
    shimmering:
You came out from the only shell you wore—espadrilles and
    shorts.

The succubus was in your room, here the sumptuous lay *sub
    verbo*—
I wonder if we do not all count upon these underlying plots:
You want the shade, the well—I want the endless summer and the
    glow.

But this we share—the inexpressible to live at ease—the surd—
I lie, subaltern, unsuborned, disarmed, unprocessed for a while,
And do not want to point at you or you the gun of any word.

How is it then that things are still so fat and fulsome for the
    knife?—
When you go home and see the faces, books, the boudoir sotte
    voce,
The sentence lashes, rips for any lucid oil, a drop of sublife.

Those lovely hours in the sun, the sentence slashed and milked to
    drouth—
I think I parse a pattern in the powers of life: Sun dogs bark
Subalterns home to open faces, books, closed lips, prim mouth.

The Clutch

If you measure your life with calipers,
The mouth of the lover may seem too thick—

It is the brush of the lips that matters,
It is the subtle engagement that counts.

Just how wide is the sea for your sources
If you think of yourself as a piston?
Go easy—push in a foot like a clutch
As if you kept a blue machine idling.

Let the touched lover see how gold and tooled
You are all over, levers at her breast,
The thrilling rub of chassis everywhere,
This interlocking sense of pause and push.

Later, in the driver's seat and bowling
Along the sea, alerted to your thrust,
You have established your intuitions,
No caroming, no crashing off the road.

I parked this image once, and let it purr,
My feet still blue in my socks, lips tingling,
Did what I could at last to calibrate
The relaxed ease of a perfect motion.

One could almost doze in this hazed hiatus,
All things still, yet powerful and throbbing,
The girl drawn close and the sleek hood shining,
The sea at the pleasure of your pedal.

One sighs as one sights the fork in the road,
Dreams of calm evening and the driftwood fire.
Is it the time, place, for disengagement,
Will the motor of the world forgive us?

I watch it all through sand-stung windshield,
Longing for singed meat and burnt marshmallows,
The red ball of the sun a beckoning—
I hear the sea murmuring for my foot.

A Charmed Life

So any mountain was his Sugar Loaf,
The sea his aphrodisiac which filled
His mind and heart only with blue stories—
This—while the silver tongs picked one small cube
For his morning coffee, the sea view culled
By the window to one strait, blue page,
The sectioned orange, diminished flotilla—
Unless one is enamored of paradox
One can never lead a charmed life, the ship
Moving in the mouth, the tongue turning the spray.
Just so, the sirens move along the veins
As the story in the window leaches,
The fingers spread out like mountain climbers,
A support group for the final assault—
It is always in the moment, the furrow
Of the future, the keel of the orange
Goes easy, launching in the avid throat;
The unruptured eye and the fineness of the fins—
There is no end of time in any vein.
One lifted finger, and the mountain soars,
The sleek savages clamor toward your tongue,
The tongs have long since loosed their measured grasp—
Of course, we discount these peaks of ecstasy,
This ravishment along the river's reach,
For something in the long run breaks the spell.
The fingers fade on the blue slope, the girls
Languish on some vague, secret rock,
The hull of the orange punctured of all juice.
Where do we go from here? I only say,
This revery at the breakfast table
Still roves and reams the impassioned detour
As if one latches on to hills, high spots—
Pips on the breast one will never spit out,
The seamless sighting of the open sea.

Private Eye

Those palms, that blue sea, which beckon through the snow:
The haunting music, those brown voluptuous girls, the fruited
    air—
How can one pierce the snowstorm with such a cameo?

Blue and green and blue again may not suffice
For those who see it every day—they plunge
A hole in it to see this land of filigree and ice.

Imagination says to an imagination: Let the others starve—
Grass skirts, dazzling beaches versus diamonded igloo:
The Sun God and The Snow Man—Everybody wants to carve!

Here in the whirling blizzard one does what one has to do—
Occlude, conclude, one has the only aperture there is:
An island lei-ed with flowers intaglioed on blue.

You rush, of course, and find the wind is steady with its brake,
The blue eye turns as heavy as a paperweight—
How could there be another cataract in every single flake?

Someone—someone stronger?—is pushing holes into the sky—
Why is one so much in a world one does not really want
Unless the islands are focussing their lapidary eye?

Touch and Go

Some day, no doubt, they may ask you: Why this?
Why that? But then you will be well beyond
Hatred and heartbreak, tugged, untuggable.
They may find you grooming the glistening sea,
Pinch it as they do luxurious stuff
But learn that it leaves, and leaves no indigo.
They may place you underneath the fabulous tree
Earringed with cherries, the woman, her cat,
How you set them there in content boudoir.
They could see your lovers fresh from the yolk

With a clear golden glaze brushed over them
As if the sun cracked an egg on the beach—
More homely, they could watch you by the fire
Teaching the clinkers to talk in a red
And bluish garden, the sinuous, muttered thing,
Or stand by the fat little boy pissing
In the fountain a solution of sources.

Why go on and on when they mean to come in,
Poke the oval, make it bleed, wipe a word
That is still damp in the blotting paper,
Lift up the necklace you put on the breast
To look for the torsion of blue and green—
Why not? What else?—the laying on of hands.
Just that the jogged sea has such savoir-faire
And remembers the fine comb in its locks.
Just that the pink cheeks, pink tongue of the cat
Chime and the wind keeps tinkling the earrings.
Ah, those lovers! How each day the sun holds
Up the handsome egg—the two, the tondo!—
I will indeed circle round and round you
Only to see what you have made of things,
Brushed also everywhere with circumspection,
The bruise bounding back from the stomach punch;
A glancing blow moves on, shooting the stars:
The reeling axis when wantons collide,
The head-on thing, the headlands enantlered.

Therefore, one cannot mind the merest touch—
The cheeks of one world against another,
The sea like a cool compress, the grasses
That sweep the skin, their lashes filled with dew.
We turn and, in time, are touched all over,
Not that we count on music of the spheres,
Or a light of love like a ruby rubbed—
Alive to shoulders listing in dark hallways:
Some must, some magic, in a sliding pause.

II

The River Boat

He loved the river boat because it was
Lazy, gentle, responded to the tides—
The different rouge of morning and sunset
As though the girl at his side tinted it.

Out for sexual adventure, they made
The river indulge them, the papyrus,
The exotic birds, the boat's slow paddle
Echoed by the shore's beast-drawn waterwheel.

Their little portable cranked out love songs
As if lovers poured through a turnstile—
One could have them naked or fully clothed:
Nothing too coarse or too fine for the needle.

The aimlessness of it all was perfect—
It gave coitus the force of a peg.
If the universe moves too forcefully,
Even a glancing kiss rips off its skin.

All that they wanted was to be buoyed
Unobtrusively and then to make love.
The boat seemed to sigh a little and pause,
Another bolt shot in its old warm flesh.

It was not to drop anchor, be master
Of when and where the voyage was over—

It was merely to mimic the flow of time,
Keeping the facts of history in steerage.

So it would seem, lover, that we put down
Our anecdotes, one peg at a time, the tent
Silken, invisible to passengers,
A skin the rippling wind cannot tear off.

Nothing like it till we hit a sandbar—
The needle jars from its close labia;
The zodiac spins its wheel of fortune,
The circuit of animals, jumped, jumbled.

One thing not foreseen—to modulate
The boat is far from easy. It pretends
To us all that it provides the slow, rich
Seductiveness of Cleopatra's barge.

It conceals that it has a nose for the shore
As if it smelled it in our warm embrace,
The swamps, the thickets, the phallic cities,
The bodies placed here, there, like paperweights.

You will remember then just how my hand
Rippled like the wind, your skirt, blouse, flowing—
The turnstile clicked shut at the threat of gale;
The zodiac tamped down its partitions.

Ah, clear night at last, so pick just one star—
We lie still as a slot machine together
We have outlasted the devious boat—
It drifts beneath us filled with shuffled signs.

Periscope

Thinking hard and feeling threatened, that day
You went up and down in your own rapt mind,
Walking upright and yet so submarine—
Meeting the woman in the field swamped you:

You lay with her in a wash of flowers,
This roll in her soft arms of a beached thing,
Back and forth still so heavy with pressure.
You remembered the raised parabola,
How the sunlight like a vertical sea
Blinded you, how she towed you, so you thought,
To safety, her pearls the richest of ropes,
The old water coming back to the mass,
The feeling that you were missing its pull—
Therefore it may well be time to crash dive,
The heart a little waterlogged but sure
To respond to its own great pump once more.
There in your mother's womb, the periscope
Looked always everywhere for you, her eyes
Folding far horizons into the blood—
How the sea knows where the throat and mouth are,
How birth is the first coming up for air,
And then, levels of green, blue, forever—
There will be great, audacious, fluid days
When you fold in your fear like an instrument.
I have discussed this matter with lovers
Who ride each other's thighs like a pent ship.
We tell each other how it feels, how one
Does not mind, persuaded of invasion,
How we sway in a blue, hypnotic song
And rise to the rainbow spill overhead.

The Torpedo

The man of many pleasures standing on the luxurious ship
Never dreamed that the sleek torpedo was rapidly approaching
    him—
He had danced, drunk champagne, held the bediamonded woman
    in his arms.

The wine sloshed a little, the woman swayed, but he braced himself
As if he let down a virile pin into the ocean's depths:
If he had spat, it would have veered then hit the bright spittoon.

Just the night before when he was a little drunk he had pitched
In his berth but no more than a heavy sandbag stopping at the
    edge—
He was too full of sex and satisfaction ever to quite fall.

All night the ring and watch which he religiously took off
Rolled in the tray but no more than a throw of dice,
Gleaming the comfortable suggestion that there would always be a
    lighthouse somewhere.

The pool on board, the table for deck tennis, the shuffleboard were
    his.
The salmon mousse lined him with his own kind of living,
The Captain saluted and acknowledged him as a genie of good
    hope.

Everyone wanted to rub against him and produce the exquisite
    day:
The boy worked his smile to arouse a better sort of father;
The dog looked at his stalwart leg and dreamed of a lamppost.

Of course, the stowaway in the lifeboat has his doubts,
The one who peeped and saw him don the abdominal belt,
    use the rouge—
Every man of pleasure in the world must have his imp.

And once in a while the woman in his arms became an incubus.
Her roving hands would pause on his chest as if to pluck out the
    hairs;
Her sex was like a seal that meant to leave some lush tattoo.

Perhaps, too, the after-dinner movie might have alerted him:
A man riding a whale in deep water, holding on for dear life
As if somehow, together, they were headed toward land to bomb
    the earth.

It may have started also when the kid turned mean and hit him in
    the stomach—
A waitress spilled a scalding dragon's blood of soup upon his neck,
The purser gave him notice on the mounting bar bill.

I who am no expert in these devastating, universal wounds
Will always admire the final and immense sangfroid
Of the man who looks up and quiets the jangling chandelier.

He can be seen in his midnight blue evening jacket, smoking at the
    taffrail
As if he will always light a little fire in the face of fate,
A false signal at the very edge of the mass of things.

Live by him and you will feel the whoosh, the released,
    languorous shiver
As the torpedo passes by, or ride with him in exploding fragments
    everywhere
As if the star you harbored in your heart remembers how the world
    began.

Screwdriver

Just because he meant for no one to put
The screws on him, the oarsman rowed so far,
So fast—The thick blue water resisting
Sometimes felt like wood close-grooved with lapis—
Back and forth in the scull as the hand does
When it turns and releases its grip,
No end to the river, no perfect fit
In the wood—the rest, an impasse always.
If lucky, you come on a scatter rug
Of water lilies, or, slow-drifting, see
A silver scab form on the rifted wake,
At least that much of the track smoothed over,
As vagary pulls and pulls the oarsman.
I have seen him bent over waiting,
Loaded with scrap iron, hands blue on the oars—
At the tip of the turn, a last idea,
As if a snake, stuck in the groove, shivered,
The backbone pushed by a screw propeller—
Perhaps no one will see the stained hands but you,
The whirling blades muffled in the world's mass
Of meanings—except, for you, no loose screws.
If the heart is a tomb of spirals, spurts,
We will forever summon out its ghosts
To plead the undelved day, the wood, the water—

I feel the driver in my flaccid pocket,
You twitch the drifting scull upon its line.

The Pier

The fruit, the flowers were gone, and now the sea
Was the place to say good-bye to summer—
As far as he could get out on the pier
Dependent though it was on poles like roots
Of rotting teeth above the blue gum line.
It creaks, mutters, promises, and he longs
To extend himself as if a brown arm
Now flung out could be an estuary
Pouring from a warm mud river inland.
The oral cavity full of the blue sea
And his own body stocked with licorice:
It is too complex—he cannot convert
These images, swaying on the pilings
Where the blue mouthwash of the water
Does not clean out the old decaying smell,
The body will not leak its sweet, damp tar.
One thing at a time. The huge pile driver
Must put a pole in place, then another,
Out into the sea, the season forgotten.
What we have is a fresh human longing,
The licorice river-man, a footing,
The nerve in the sapphire socket,
A quick, blinding pain when the driver hits—
I can give you then the simple sadness:
Suddenly an exposed root in the air,
The props all gone, only the pier swaying—
Soon autumn with its overrich gold fillings
Will make some sort of tomb with each inlay.

The Winged Eye

I had come to the end of everything, the black sky,
The crows, red berries like a touch of blood,
When over the ship of death fluttered a winged eye.

For this is what it seemed, moving out, on, much too far,
The sense of a masked, red figure standing in the prow—
I have no other way to tell you what late autumns are.

It is as though the rose reneged, the fruits were all self-ravished—
One has these human but delusive ways of talking to the world:
How could the rose wish to die on whom my love was lavished?

Why did the fruit destined for my tongue dare to show a spot?—
It is as though a lover, fondled and fondled, claimed at last,
Said in a smoky, late-autumnal voice: I would rather not.

This is where—at least I think it does—the eye with wings
Hovers over red-draped figure and the falling leaves,
And says: You do not have a corner on all lovely things.

I am the one suspended in your dreams whether or not you know.
The ship was always full of fruits, flowers, now with leaves, men in
    red—
Here are wings. Look back into the mind again before you let the
    summer go.

III

The Trellis

So there I was lying in my breechcloth
While the scented trade winds blew over me,
Stripped clean of angst by a swim in the sea,
My skin air-brushed with the gold of the sun—
Somewhere, far off, the image abattoir
As I stretched out dreaming with open hands,
No hammer, no cleaver, no dripping club,
Blood in the eyes transferred to hibiscus—
One learns these extrapolations early,
The use of the salve and the saving grace,
The flinging oneself down at the day's end,
Calling amorini from the smogged air,
A woman's perfume floating a garden—
Done before, so we can do it again.
It is as though you harbor an ideal man
Who always waits like a nonpaying guest.
Give him a bed by the sea to flourish,
A sunset suit in the rich evening light.
Still one is struck with the fact that he is
Put down—a glancing blow of the hammer?—
The optic nerves in the thread of a flower,
In the soft hand, the ghost of a handle?—
He wants to pay his keep with your content,
Offering his chest to your late mistress,
Suggesting balneologies of blue,
How the demulcent trade winds treat the lips,

The *aequo animo* of his undress.
He is a trellis of the treasured life.
But one cannot quite get over the fact
That he is fallen, that some blow did tell,
His heart ravished with its own red roses,
The lattice of last resort, espaliered nerves.
One rests and rests—at last, supine success.
Whether it was wind, will, or wayward love,
You were pushed over in a pose—I come
Along the beach, stuffed with this fantasy:
No wonder it fell, no wonder it fell!—
Unless we finger forays one at a time,
Feeling the nerve faint in the golden man,
The cravings that cram from the crosspieces,
Even the lying down is too lonesome—
Who can say the tyrant of the trellis
Does not plan, pitch, a tower in the sand?

In Cold Blood

You come up naked like something destined for a platter,
Some seaweed clinging, a trace of primal lettuce salad,
Stretch out, the sun's fresh meal, taken from deep-refrigerated
      water.

But you do not mean at all to really satisfy,
Repeating some atavistic ritual of the first Man-Fish
Who had no sacrificial thought of crawling on the land to die.

Self-cleaned of scales, you may indeed present the aspect of a feast,
A quiet creature breathing furtively against the ground,
Just beyond the grasp of that enormous blue-tongued beast.

Who shall have you is the question, cold or hot—
There are only two forthright primordial choices
Which promulgate cuisine—the conscious warmth, the gelid
      figure you forgot.

But, for a moment, lying comestibly upon the beach,
You are a deliriously delicious double creature,
Attractive to the sun and sea and flatly claimed by each.

A hand, an arm, a foot, is given to the sun
Much as you offer tidbits to a tender god:
The rest is blue-belonging fish quite sometimes upon the blazing
    sand may leave half done.

The Sun Says Grace

Lying naked on the long diving board,
You imagine the sun will nod to you,
That great, wondrous head without a body—
You are so simply and utterly there,
Semi-soft and ambiguously hard—
Suddenly your own head simmers, takes fire.
You rise and stand saluting the hot face;
You imagine how often that has occurred,
This intimate appeal for recognition,
A man lighting his oiled brain like a flare,
Writing a poem, a story, making love,
Looking first to that stark, cerebral glare
As if it loved a torso that it did not have—
Unless you believe that you have something
The sun loves, an utterance, an amorous hand,
You will not prosper long in this bright world—
Thus I can cast the young man upon the board,
Filled with his loose, relaxed recognitions;
Even his casuistry is commodious,
An intimacy so powerful and fine
The violation of a passing cloud
Cannot quite erase the warm, solar smile—
I have an enormous and worldwide sense
Of just what some such close rapport can do—
I lie on the board as if it were a stalled spit,
So much on this side—turn—so much on that,
A morsel for the manners of the sun.

Vulcan at Sunrise

It ebbs at night perhaps, but in the morning ego flows anew—
Green pajamas drop, peel off. The molten and metallic man
Goes down to the sea to do battle royal with that blue.

The fierce emotions are contained ironically in golden-glow.
It is as though a small volcano shaped like a suntanned man
Positioned itself at water's edge, ready with a lava-flow.

You know how full you can be of last night's left-over lover or
    lust—
I have stood naked on the beach, and felt so golden, golden,
As if any minute I would erupt with sunflower-bright volcanic
    dust.

There is, of course, some sibilance in this—
The sea advances with its blue tongue curled:
You seethe, fume with your fantastic fire, the blue waves hiss.

One takes the first step forward, lined with brilliance and
    containing tons—
The sea, that enormous, everlasting cooking element,
Accepts the molten, manic foot, and makes it bronze.

Brushed with patina, a leg, a thigh, the chest, the head,
I love this beautiful, quiet, morning hour, cooling off,
No longer so disruptive—for liquid fire, this figure of a man
    instead.

Up Close and Personal

Pour water into the percolator
Filled with fine grounds of lapis lazuli:
Perhaps it will give you a cup of the sea.
Lance and peel the tightly wound golf ball—
Could it hold the final source of pictures,
The pure, packed message of the flight of birds?
Keep molten sunset, keep it in the heart:

Will you lie like an ingot in your bed?
Even a skewer run through raw meat
Drips into the ecstatic nerves of fire,
And the fat blazes up its reprisals.
I am saturated, impacted, impaled:
Sea-veined, gold in the flesh, a rich, stuck thing—
The loveliest silk woman at the cookout
Has no idea at all what she deals with,
Though her jeweled pin with its concealed, fine point
Contributes a subtle understatement—
The wine in her glass, the color of bruised sea,
Fondled white beads that could serve as a lifeline.
So one stands, stoked, stuck, with a long lifetime
Of longing, sensing a slow, blue dripping
In the ear, hearing the struck golf ball whirr,
Regretting the stiff, golden nights alone.
How can we stand so close to each other
Except that the point thrusts, and the fire flares,
And we hope for supple, sunset idols?—
I feel that pin on her breast, warm, pressing:
It is like fate that's still subtilizing,
Subtilizing—You never can quite say
If the crushed sea is coursing in her veins,
Or the fat fire has finished its suttee.

The Spool

It may be hidden, of course, a blue spurt
In an hysterical vein when the sea
Makes an obscene, groping overture
And you are felt all over by the cold,
Afraid to be alone with nature.
It could be caterpillars dropped on your face
In the garden, excrement of the sky—
Do the trees waste such creatures on you?
Damage control sets in, and a warm hand
Woos the water—a support group of swimmers
Dive and give the cold sea their goldshots.
Though a personal sadness is inseminated,

Babies of ebullience are never blue.
A worm is better than egg on your face;
Lakes of the eyes shimmer futurity:
Leave life alone a bit, and wings may rise.
These little piercing dramas every day:
A stitch in the side means the universe
Is sewing, jaggedly perhaps, but keen.
Even sunset's glorious golden cloth runs
With red as if the needle always bleeds
As it pulls and pulls you toward the night.
So now you know that you must wet the thread,
Warn the sea, warm and warm the hapless worm.
It is no small thing to observe oneself
Making an eye of everything, ogives
Of regret and happiness. Drops of spit
Mellow in the mouth. It would take a dredge
To raise the projected pictures. So lie
At night, stuck, resting in a spool of silk.

The Turn-On

Just breaking the blue skin of the calm sea,
Using yourself as a gold swizzle stick
As if you meant to stir fresh concoction,
As though the world needed a deep blue cocktail,
The unsieved thing, swirling sand and gravel,
As if you had plated yourself in the sun
Just for this, undaunted dasher at dawn—
Why not say you have this dervish passion?

Why not speak of these extreme relations?—
How you stand bolt upright in a flower bed
And think what it is to mix earth's palette,
A coat of many colors as you turn,
This full, rich leaching-out of oils
So that a stone calls to you for lithograph—
You could follow the lead of the fountain
And gush forever with pentimenti.

Even your hand on the waist of a lover
Is the first signal to ravel the rose,
The sheath, the undergarments, the shedding,
As if sex itself were a centrifuge.
Why not say that you desire everything
And sorrow itself is a grindstone:
Something whetted every time you turn around,
The shimmer of dust, the shower of sparks.

This much and more this morning drips from you
As you stand from stirring the taste of the sea.
Inland, grapes are calling blue to brown feet:
Hitched up dresses, the circling in the vat—
You may have my grindstone as a discus—
I can see it whirling, whirling in the sun.

The Hinge

In late summer these desires, back and forth,
Call up the subtlest of our scents and oils
As if one rutted with the rose in hand,
One last time touched the skin with golden glaze.
We look in the garden for its blood-drops,
Impatiens scattering red petals like stigmas,
The sun demanding the cross too often.
Someone with blue feet coming home from the sea
Jams the door of the bathing house to see
Us hanging wet suits on rusty nails,
The body-varnish showing its seams, cracks,
These versions clashing on a swinging door—
It is perfectly true the bee does not
Seek us out for nectar, nor wish
Even to sting us anymore. We lie
Bejeweled by the pool, and the mild sun
Has no lust to rob us of salt diamonds—
I do not wish to lead you at this time,
But let you linger here, there, this way, that:
The rose, the rough jumble of sea and pool,
The bee on missions exclusive of us,

The impatiens increasing stigmata.
So the season gives us split decisions—
The car comes back with some sand on the floor,
A few shells turned up like calcified ears
That still listen for the sea behind us.
Those cattails in a vase are the flails
Of the marsh to drive us back next summer,
All winter, a blue pennant in the mind.
One day here, one day there, a grab bag swings—
The shower pours down the chest like paint remover,
The feet grow tall into that new blue suit,
And the last rose falls to the greedy sea:
This heave of images is now unhinged—
It is time, at last, to oil the autumn.
I see the greased tools spread out in the sun.
The whetstone seems to tell us—Give me words:
Next time a lapidary in your mouth.

The Afterworld

Summer goes again, and you release its fable—
Tanned swimmers in blue pools, blue seas, the spectres of fading
    roses,
The glistening lust for life, the predator at table.

All the lovers, all the grapes and melons that you knew—
I kissed the girl, ate the fruit with her,
And fantasized that melon rind offered voyages of love in its canoe.

The thing we like the most is just the thing that keeps on coming
    after—
The caressive sun on skin made stringent by the pool,
The comic songs from sentimental ones, from those romantic tears
    the sparkling laughter.

This is what the fable says, this is what it does for us:
Pears come after peaches, melons. The hammock, packed with
    power,
Sways and sways—a basket for late pathos.

Or so it was, to me, in early June related.
Such relatives that came to picnic on my lawn!—
The muscled one looked like Apollo, the predator was never sated.

Still, in moonlight, comes a time for one last, rueful kiss:
Gold figures folded in the pool, blue worlds we fully occupied—
The afterthought is asking now if tales of autumn hold anything
    like this.

IV

River Job

The man sitting by the smooth, blue tablecloth
Longed for summer, the rush of the river,
Wished that the cloth would make waves, show bruises
Of purple, dose the house with liquidity—
He gagged, swallowed hard from keeping so much back,
Lepered the surface with a few wine spots,
And then let it beg once more for bounty.
From such a source as this all rivers flow:
Blue flashes in the mind, the groin engorged,
Water-shadows shaking on the ceiling,
A strong need to swallow an emetic—
No deep current moves without this pressure,
Spends too fast, leaves only damp and mudstains
On the table, the thin trickle downstream,
Bathers stranded without a drop of blue.
Still, it may be an eternal question
Whether rivers do not rot when they rest,
Closed in the dark calyx of tight delta—
Let us suppose the man's symphonic best:
The house bulging and the great dam far off,
The moment when we first rumple forward,
The dried mud baking in the brilliant sun,
The nude bathers waiting in ecstasy.
I have had traffic with these river-gods
And let them ripple my life at will—
There is nowhere a massage quite like it,

Tense sinews, muscles, milked for miles of blue—
Then one rises, having been worked over,
And sits in the man who rolls the river up.

The Aquarium

All of the fluid, it seemed, had been sucked from the room,
The spongy blue chairs, the shell-like objects on the desk were
    high and dry:
Nothing was left of the sea but the small aquarium.

The blue eyes of the man in the room could hardly wink,
Had he seen the sea into this subjection,
His bibulous art dependent on a hidden bottle of ink?

As though it might be home for silver fish, the mirror
Refuses to waver, becomes a monstrous oblong cenotaph:
One does not break and enter tombs without a certain ruffian
    sense of terror.

Still, the man can flounder just two steps and get a cramp.
Certain things extend the jagged, cruel touch of coral,
And fumbling with his shoes that seem enmired, he finds his socks
    are damp.

The aquarium, then, must be engaged head-on, clear-blind—
The lasciviously tinted shells, little turning wheel, arrogant
    bubbles,
Suggest crashing storms dehydrated almost too safely from the
    mind.

Curiously, rounding the wheel, the silver fish come on to thank
The man for standing there in silence like a pump,
As though an artifice could dread the large inclosure of a dried-up
    tank.

The Swamp

That long summer the man was feeling somewhat damp—
There were roses, but they seemed to bloom from mists:
Was he living in a neighborhood rather like a swamp?

He did not want to think too ill of life, have thoughts too harsh
Of those who came to see him only in the moonlight
Just when the will-o-the-wisps were gathering on the marsh.

One woman, the very loveliest of them all,
Who brought him a rose with the chill of fog on it,
Seemed to say: I live this side, and you, beyond the pall.

In later years, would he see it as the most romantic summer
    ever?—
Moonlight, roses, and yet this fetor in the air,
As if gas were always rising, infecting him with something like
    swamp fever.

One must be an idealist, living near the spongy grass, the constant
    wet—
You cannot let the rose go silver in the head,
Or give the lovely woman nothing more than moonlight and
    regret.

One may not ever be quite rid of this estate,
The smell of gas, the sound in the trees like the sewing of a shroud,
But look again, oh look again—sunrise tints the rose, her hand is
    on the gate.

Wall Fountain

The imperial lion has lost his head
Flowing water instead of blood,
Green-mouthed as if he understood
The silent, virile things he might have said.

Perhaps a sickly moment but what verse
Would want this image gone forever,
The father-figure of a river
Which waits the lifting of a curse?

The rick-rack in the kitchen, the little hum
Of furtive lovers in the bower
Still simulate the finest hour
Of men who bring some monster to his doom.

We keep our images in trust—
The naked marble nymph for just that day
The satyr in us held at bay
Gleams like a sword redeemed from rust.

Thus, lovers who feel some sad lack
At last, missing some bright mountain,
May sit and hear the music of the fountain
As though a lion were roaring at their back.

White Lake

When he considered where to vacation,
He first constructed a lacustrine house,
Cool as a glass of iced water, yet bright,
Clear, as if lighted by a diamond,
Intermittent, blinking on a woman's hand.
His libido somewhere swallowed silver
And found expression in this broad expanse,
The lake going out to the horizon
As if drawn by white birds on noiseless wings,
Pulling this long, liquid, inner mirror
Into matrix of which it did not know.
He could lie in the house, eat *langue de chat*,
Smell the lilies, imagine lianas,
Since the white cottage could be anywhere,
Insisting on their lifting, slow embrace—
The kind of house where one can pad around
In drawers or nothing, a silver agent
At ease in little but a signet ring,

Those who have swallowed their share of those coins
Made from misapprehension's mother lode
Are glad to sit like Buddha argentine,
Knowing lake lotus has positioned them,
The cool navel chaliced for sweat
Should the sun work for vermeil through the slats.
Therefore, when you are making travel plans,
Consider the id, whether the lucent stretch,
Waterfalls, mountains, or the open sea—
Vacations, unless somewhat instinctive,
Bring the zombie into the harsh sunlight,
Waiting for silver leis beside the lake.

Claws

So there it was in my clear waking dream,
The rich nude struggling in a lobster's claw:
The mini-figure, minatory light.
One could see a little necklace dangling,
A bracelet—who was it tagged the tortured?
One has a sense of the tools of the trade,
Pliers, prods, and then this most natural thing,
The body caught in a claw like a finger.

I have nothing to say in my defense
When things like this well up into the mind:
The bruise on the thumb where the hammer struck,
The look of lacerations on the wrist—
This meat surfaced from the aquarium's murk
As if one went fishing with a phallus.
She dazzles in the light, those blinking tags:
How can a monster make a show of medals?

One could, of course, throw up a wry disguise,
Offering a crate of artificial eyes
That can be rolled to any point of view—
Here in isolation, let me enlarge
At least—the sharp grasp smoothed from my arms—
I dance with her, the imperious relieved.

She has him now, a man made up of tears:
How could that tiny sea contain such salt?

The Crane

You may have the egret if you will let me have the crane—
That symbol of good fortune and long life has been
For longer than I remember wading in my brain.

The little house surrounded by bamboo, the blue lake,
Need just this serious bird calmly stalking there
To tell me what I wanted all these years was no mistake.

In the house I really live in, really own and know,
I want a sometime refuge, drawn, perhaps, by Hokusai,
As if the heart were always beating round a secret cameo.

You have every right to chandelier, fan, plume, egret—
I love them too in many moods except this secret one
Which comes from moving in an aura, tone of the bird's-foot
    violet.

I like the rough-and-tumble, the rub of hardy fellows,
But in the twilight, I can feel the heart gathering, coalescing,
Its circular relief—the bird is standing in the shallows.

An hour, an evening, before *lex talionis* must assert its right—
Is this how we come at all to notions of good fortune, long life:
The plash, the long, slow steps in the water, until the crane takes
    flight?

The Towline

When you see a spectacle of nothing,
Be glad when something powerful obtrudes:

A stalk of lilies brought into the house,
The brilliant yellow throats and orange tongues,
These megaphones that mock the nihilist.
It is as though they had been lifted up
And out of life for just this stark meeting:
White vacant light everywhere—still, still life,
As if it offered no other refuge,
As though the flesh of the earth had been flailed,
Somewhere in the void the loose skin of things—
One bends, works up the world a bit from scent,
Sticks out the tongue toward the bright orange dust
As if language should be rolled in lavishness,
Impoverishment repaired in a mellow mouth.
Let me tell you lives can be built anew
On one such image. I have seen it happen
In a lonely room—the hostel, the hospice,
The powerful summoned and obtrusive thing.
I have seen the glorious sun coming back,
The skin returning moist and glistening—
First the musk of the marsh and then the sea.
I am perfectly aware the lily
Drops like a skin to the floor, shrivels, dies,
The orange is washed down by the mouthwater,
The lush word must wade on into shallows.
Still, give me lilies in a lonely room—
Each time we match a powerful obtrusion,
I think we twitch and tow the cosmos back.

The Swan at Sunset

It is late. Shall I have one long, last look at the swan
As it moves on the river, sluicing its purity,
Or simply say—never, never in this world will it be done?

One wants something else, another more exciting part—
A second nature to rise in the orange beak, stab
And stab again until a sunflower opens in the heart.

I have had this counter-urge perhaps more often than I know.
Wanting a thing to be itself yet come at me like a sunburst
As I stand on the banks, waiting for the powerful orange glow.

Once more, then, the impeccable purity and the brilliant skewer
Just as the image darkens, goes down to dross, detritus,
As though the brain of man, at last, floats on a sewer.

It is so late. Can one now, in fact, rethink—
The palace, the palm trees, the bird sowing on the river—
Must I let go, throw the ultimate sunflower down into the sink?

Or simply say: An orange glow. A swan has passed me by—
How many times have I felt so full as this, a face of seed,
As if I would go on, flowering and flowering, against the splendid
    sky?

The House on the Hill

Was it the caged bird or the blue curtains
That we remember most?—that master scene:
The white bed with its rich, lace coverlet,
The pictures of nudes that looked like mirrors—
In another room the stored viscera,
The offal extracted from the absurd,
Ready to leach into the adored place.
This is simply to tell you that not all
Moments are "equal," that passion and power
May be divided, that a sorrow came
Into the world and we built our houses—
That we sort out our procedures
As soon as we take possession of the white
Room and the red, searching the spotless rug
For the first seam of blood, a reaching nerve,
Blotting the stain with a silk-stockinged foot.
So far, open house would be indecent
Unless you cram your friends in a tight space,
Some who favor the white, and some, the red.
We love those masterbuilders who permit

No compromise with a pervasive style
And who relegate the rest to closets,
The caged bird balancing the deep closure,
The sea wind pushing the blue curtains like sails,
The beautiful lovers happily enlaced.
Of course, some days the house will hang heavy
As if it wore a blood blister, a pouch
On its side ready to burst, flood outward
Into the city and into the news—
What are headlines for but lancing the soul?
Meanwhile, we may have conquered the ground plan:
That calm stroll from one room to another,
Somewhere, way in the back, a love story:
Remember those people who lived on the hill?

V

Water Wings

Too bad about the wax, but Icarus
Should have known his father was not perfect—
The sea is harder than it ever looks,
Pocked with meshing sapphires, secret boulders.

One needs in any case support systems:
A sense for landing where the waves are plush,
Someone in a canoe there just by chance,
Sea polyps standing in for water wings.

One or all of these unless you should have
A flawless nose for that daedal cunning.
For you will fall more than once—that for sure—
Even your dreams have warned you since childhood.

Smells of burnt jam call for the coiled hose:
The odor of an unwashed lover makes
You wonder if she set the house on fire—
Where are the exit stairs from this suttee?

Too bad when you had your first plunge you did
Not know the rock pools were sucking the sea,
The tit removed twice a day—While it flowed,
You could have floated in on mother's milk.

I know for I have seen Icarus walk
Away from it with just the sunburn marks

On his shoulder blades like bad memories
Of too much trust and those parental blunders.

I have seen him regroup his sore muscles,
Oiling and preening in the brilliant light,
Watching the bulging amniotic sac,
Still pregnant from his nearly fatal dive.

Ah, mother, mistress, the sliding sea
Cannot lay hands upon him any more
Or try to leave blue babies at his feet—
The condom on the sand is his congé.

It is time for cabana or kiosk,
The saline mouth washed out with pink fruit ice,
And the vendor tells you where the girls are,
Smiles, leers a little as he calls you, "Son."

For that predictable fall into bed,
One cannot ape the practice of our peers,
Those famous lovers and their bruises, salves,
Their arms printing and printing the moulting wings.

So shall I lie on the hard floor at least
And wish it might be richly sluiced with sweat?—
When nothing lifts up the heart, slip or slide
Back to the sea where once you learned to fall.

Loose Ends

Somehow he must relocate the center
Which would not hold—the sapphire dissolving
To blue sugar, the rose in the paperweight
Full-blown in his hand as he dashed it down,
A contrived thing in its tight crystal womb—
The chipped buttons sagging from his jacket,
A raveling thread in his thin underwear
As if, secretly, he were pulled apart.

But you can cite your own diaspora:
The cold wave drawing, sucking back from you
As if it took a ripe fruit from your groin,
The lover's head coming in like flotsam,
Rolling on your chest all kisses spent.
The flaming clouds, the skywriting, fade—
This, perhaps worst of all, such bold language,
With nothing graven except the gravestone.

Small wonder we take our knockout drops,
Overinhaling the rose so it will hold,
Remembering the glass splinters on the floor—
Drain glass after glass of wine for gem-silt—
Pout a pin in the eye of the button,
Tie a loop in the head of the thread-worm—
I see you at sunset, hoping for star words
That blink in the trail of invisible ink.

I have no other comradeship to give
When the last diamond peels from the ring
And drops like a white seed in the darkness.
You hitch a ride one way, I another.
Somewhere the new garden will be centered;
It is not always autumn everywhere.
Even the flung paperweight makes compost,
Even the lolled head will be anchor-lulled.

You have bruised, purple night, I its splinters,
A string in the navel, a pulling hand—
At each new signpost, at least the flashlight.
I take this to be somewhat the answer:
The face at the lip of the undrained glass,
At my feet the sprouted diamond. We do
Not altogether fail to fling our foci,
Lifting syntax from letters on the grave.

The Wisteria Sailor

Mentally, the man had come to the end of the road.
His mind felt like a mash of squashed dreams,
The succulence of disaster, a tumor of doubts accrued.

No wine, fermenting liquor, for it all lacked fire—
The silent hearer, who remembers inclosing cataracts,
Listens, drop by drop, to the climacteric of desire.

So this is the impacted life, the final, futile, hoard,
He is sick as a full ship without wind and water:
Subject to object cried, once too often, "Man overboard!"

And yet no one is more intent upon escape—
He resuits his dreams like costume-buccaneers,
Presses at each thought as if pumping a deflated grape,

Makes of himself an embattled literary situation, indulges in
    rhetoric.
What if he can remand the mutinous crew from cannibal islands
And the stuff of life around him is nowhere canvas-thick?

But spring acts as if it knows just what his malady entails:
Swathes of wisteria hung from brute pine staffs
Force the man on his back to take on purple sails.

The Fling

Such a ferocious longing for the sea,
Gymnast that you are in sleek white suit,
Your hot head crammed only with blue hours,
Wanting a sea-smell under your armpits,
Hoping each package that comes in the mail
Is saltwater taffy pulled by veined hands—
You would like to lash the fountain with your tongue
If it would beg for mercy with blue wine.

114

So what can you say of yourself—that you
Have eaten and eaten diamond dust, slept
Between milk-white sheets, Atlas albinoed?—
That you wake, race to the indigo mouthwash,
Swear at the mangle for flattening the cloth
So that dreams could not pitch in a sea-swell?—
The shadows in the mirror as you shave confirm
The block of which you are a chip is blue.

Still, white underwear, knee bends, push-ups
Condone the desire at least to go out picking
Blueberries, write blue notes to a stranger,
The girl who would pass them on to the sea—
These appetites are seldom singular.
Therefore one makes way for the unassuaged
Offering their tongues to the doctor's paddle
As if it were a fathom—an anchor somewhere,
A ballast of bluestone in the belly.
We look for each other's fingernail disks
As if once in a blue moon we will find
The sea throwing its loose chips everywhere.

So in this great banter of obsessions,
I find these inland mornings do not pall
And do not pale in much comparison.
Our lips will have a trace of foam on them;
The cleaning lady with her slops is sure
She leaves a floor of sapphire in her wake.
Together, let us go today, next week—
The sea will be fulsome with our fragments
Because we put such chisels to our dreams.

Islands Beyond A

The man, Everyman's late, last, cousin felt trapped, walled up
    alive, interred—
You have seen him at the tombstone of his dictionary:
Where is the world that lies well beyond the Word?

How can one turn the heavy page among the Bs,
And find the blue that was the sea before we gave it any name,
Skip over toward the end and find our first perception of the trees?

Someone, of course, has saved up for this man a fruit
Which has not been through any funeral of the mind,
And smiles with its red lips as though, not having ever spoken, it is
    never mute.

Someone else has even hoarded up a human face,
Fresh as a flower, beyond all nomenclature:
No ethnic origin, no designated time, no master race.

She, if anyone, can make him throw away the book
And watch it, still unsinkable—the pages ruffled, a convulsive
    raft—
See some final word like lover give back an agonizing look.

A fruit, a face, that language never touched informs the hand
Ambiguously to save and save, and throw away,
Clutching every shipwreck to the heart and pulling to another
    land.

Dipstick

He had wanted to be immersed in life:
Into the sea like a dipstick in blue,
Into the batter, a bloated raisin,
Into the cream, a lascivious tongue—
The nude in the choker—would she prefer
To be buried up to her neck in pearls?
The wine sop longs and longs for the weir,
A finger, pulled from the pudding, fevers.
One wants to enter, enter, not withdraw:
Fruits, heaped on the sideboard, all pies deep-dish.
The canoe is towed by the waterfall,
The naked skin cannot resist the kiss.
Into the morass and into the murk

116

To rescue a legend of the limpid:
The sea diaphanous to our desire,
The aurora held up in the wine glass,
The woman conceived as mother of pearl—
Just this morning, this thick, heady brew,
This slew, this great puncturing of pictures,
A wanting to come up somehow coated,
To center in the rising arabesque,
Shedding a shower of jonquils, hyacinths,
Drenched in the full, drawn-down, liquids of spring—
It is not every day that one can feel
This way, the pump somehow idle of all thrill—
The tongue dripping a single drop of cream,
The sea in its great, wide, blue flatulence
Unstirred by gold swan dives into its side,
The choker, a dog collar of desire.
Come, ecstasy, come, whenever you can:
The lips will swell to yielding cabochon,
Deep, deep, the stick is stable in the oil.

The Vise

Remember that blue day by the full sea
When you wanted to match it with your love?—
The diapason of desire, the hand,
Then the gold body entering the water,
The jaws of the vise opening forever.
Somewhere out of sight, of course, the iron
Lies idle, the screw is tensing again—
The sea heaves as if pressed for some extract,
Even the rocks squeezed like balls in a sack.
Your last headache held hard without fenders—
Therefore this pushing is so passionate,
Like Atlas, akimbo, holding back harm,
The sun lifting its hammer from your head,
The lungs pneumatic, testicles floating—
I have long studied the vagaries of the vise,
How one side will seem to move first, bruising
The cheek, the iron wanting its lover,

A hard movement below as of leg irons—
Therefore whenever equal sides caress you,
Bathe, swim in an equilibrated sea,
Stretch out on the beach and suck a jujube,
The stuffed lockjaw delivered of its pearls,
The golden body supple as a chain.
I have told so many: Push, part, partake,
Use a chisel on the mouth if need be,
As if the first effusion were your blue rinse
And the sea loved the water of your tongue—
No matter if sunset finds you wriggling
At the hot touch of embrasure closing:
You will have learned such a turning technique
That somehow sea and summer match the heart.

The Art of Quotation

I quail, I do not really acquiesce, but still deliver shocks—
I remember when a powerful, pungent blue wave like volcanic
    undercurrent
Pushed me off my feet and, as if it had turned lighter-than-air,
    threw my body against the rocks.

I was proud of my metallic arms, the mettle in my brain,
Had even fantasized that I would stand, withstand,
If modern cities fell be one of those, when centuries passed,
    dredged up whole where I had lain.

The blue punch, the red blood flowing cured me of that trope—
Some rings appeared upon my hands, a red necklace snaked and
    snaked around my skin—
The sea struck again as if blue robbers never cease to interlope.

It gave me such a savage beating, so senseless that it had its sense.
It knew that it could take its full, sadistic toll,
And without a solid citizen in sight remove the evidence.

I did what Conrad might have done, advising me of fate,
Or how you must act hugged by the voracious bear:

118

Do not counterpunch just then. Do the impossible. Wait.
     Surrender as deadweight.

The blue hug, blasé at last, released me, cleaned, no longer
     bleeding, to myself.
I must get up, go down again, my mind a jar of images—
I do not write in red, nor live for shocks, but have a blue contained
     to sometimes ink the epigraph.

Blue Blazes

A long way to a garden or the sea,
An oasis tucked in behind some dunes—
Though it is hot as blue blazes, you walk,
Dreaming mirage, the sedan chair swaying.

Still, the heated mind leaches these notations:
A swing on a vine in the deep forest,
A waterfall, your own voluptuous chute,
The swoon when your bottom lands on thick moss.

I have seen men staggering in the sun,
Back, forth, hallucinating the floral censer,
The tongue curling in on its mouth water,
The picture of borne pallet, dehydrated man.

We cannot refrain, we must torch ourselves,
Calling to the nude girl to oil our way,
Cringe when the dry wind instead licks our skin—
The sand guards its brazier under the stars.

Comes laconic morning—the rope made of sheets,
The rushed escape down your cooling passions—
In the haze, the parked cars like sedan chairs:
You will be carried over simmering roads.

Still, the lighter on the dashboard flares up,
There's a glitter of sand on the floorboard.

The smudged sneakers belong to the firebrand,
Nothing but warm spit in last night's used flask.

I tell myself this fable on summer days:
The sliced melon ready to shoot the rapids,
My tongue let out to lavish a fresh world,
Aware of the heaped up, heaped in, conglomeration.

Clothes blow on the line, the spigot flumes,
Any minute I light a cigarette
As a signal of my depredation,
A sign to the blue flame in the distance.

Can we ever pull it out of the fire?—
One takes lip-salve from the rose, one simmers
In lucidity—the ignis fatuus:
I see it flashing in the swaying skull.

VI

Land's End

If you follow the sunset long enough, you
Will come to land's end, a view of the sea.
Does anything remain of the old savage?—
This brilliant flare remembered from the caves,
How it spread and spread each day like the fan
Of your nature, the faculae of fate.
A man carries a torch toward sundown,
Lifting it up to see the painted world,
Having early a sense of afterglow
Like a peacock tail, sensation's bright trail—
Thus we wear our fine feathers to the end,
Or hope we do, moulting and moulting by torchlight,
Aware of inscribed pictures so far back,
The pulled, and pulled-out, inside of our life,
A walking fossil in the dying light.
If happiness is a kind of flourishing,
A flaring on and on toward sunset,
I need not even caution the cave man
In whose heart surely all ecstasy begins—
I know indeed the dropped and the drooped feather,
How the figure drawn with a burnt stick dims,
The folded fan of our fascination,
The broad sweep uncentered by a ruby light.
Before, I hope, the sunset of sunsets,
I come to the edge, stand like a colored stone,
The afterglow stalled and the future stilled,

The torchlight doused in a rich, deep dreaming—
Another picture shudders in the dusk.

The Man with the Blue Spine

Not knowing what the day would bring, caring immensely, but
    fearful too,
He had a strange columnar, yet branching, sense of himself,
A secret psychosis of extension, as if his spine were blue.

Was it conspiracy or callousness that others did not stare?—
Here was a man hung from a stagy, startling, synaptic crux,
This shadowy thing, both stiff and supple, which holds him in the
    air.

The day might be warm, easy-sliding, to those in gold and tan—
In this way, most days are rather warm—We walk the beach,
Simmering our identities a little as they melt like butter in a pan.

But there in our straight and stricken man these azure mists
Which fall and fall like moisture of a multifoliate place
Where, so I am told, in the vagaries of a cistern, his body-tree
    persists.

Good God, we must permit somehow that image, essence,
    overlap—
We cannot have mere easy oil across a sliding picture,
And who would only settle for the blue, miasmal, spinal tap?

We live on a brilliant beach and in this forest of recessive trees,
Humped together: Wait a moment—the burn sinks beneath the
    butter,
And there is nothing cooling in the world but blue leaves falling in
    an arid breeze.

The Vigneron

The railing with its tendrils and black leaves,
Climbing vegetation stalled by the plague,
Wavers at least on the brilliant blue pool
As if the burnt chlorophyll awakened
Might capriciously bloom in the water,
Exquisite blue flowers on curled black stems—
The man on the balcony leans over,
Prepares to cultivate this blue garden.

The world must revere its wrought-iron fences,
Placing them near to lovers and graveyards,
Harsh cummerbunds for the living and dead.
One presses against them at groin level,
The vegetative lust between the legs,
A spike impaling the bluest love-ghost,
The cigarette smoke coughed up in anguish
From the deep innertube of indigo.

Nevertheless, wait for the vine to climb,
Teach the pool oceanic ambitions,
A hidden bag of sapphire for your seed—
Meanwhile, the modern fantasy arrives:
A circus man dives in a tank of fire,
In one fell swoon, the deep, fertile furrow—
I have seen these men wipe off flame like hair,
Depilated, heavy with natural fruit.

Squeeze Play

It may be the cold water of the sea
That leaves its blue tattoo upon the glans,
The charley horse that strikes the golden thigh
Just as the champion runner hits his stride—
Or the little, secret drama of desire
When the lover states her own conditions.

The pullback has the strange effect of pressure:
You feel naked, flattened against the wall,

Your fullness now totally espaliered.
The warning: Grow thinly and more sparely;
Don't look too rich, hung with fruits of pleasure,
A Giacometti man hides in us all.
I have seen the swimmer, blue in the light,
The cramped runner doubled over in grief,
The lover slapped around by the snapback
When the one pushed against the wall lets go.

We love the home stretch and the honing in
On contradictions of the lucid day:
The swimmer all flushed with the blood's revenge,
The winner finding breath for the victory lap,
The lovers' full, clutched, soaring monody—
Nevertheless, a last accordion note:
The stars tonight look pressed in perfect poise—
One falls, the phantom of a cosmic loss.

The Child of Life

So you have had enough and are filled, flooded,
Breast fed by the sea, rain infiltrated,
All those ruts and gulleys no one can see—
How can you hold that last cup of blue wine
Like a nipple of the sea stemmed on glass?
How can the creased groin manage the run-off,
The tongue take one more dewdrop from the lily?—
A look at the waves and your gorge rises.
The first signs could be cankers on your lips:
The ground water is rapidly climbing.
Then that luxurious sweat in the arms
Of a lover, the overplus of ardor,
At the end, to lie in a golden pool.
You rise, look at the mirror, all aglow
As though a solution of daffodils
Had been priming the power of contact.

Food after love, and the rapturous, ripe peach
Will drown, go under the mouth water,
The love-death swoon as the fruit slice slides down.
Ask yourself if this is not your first desire
That no sensation should ever escape you:
A copious spirit standing behind you,
Pouring and pouring over your shoulder,
The complexion of the jaundiced mirror clearing.
I say this, hating the blisters, skin-blight—
The pale orphan hiding in the mirror
Who never struggled from the silver swamp.

The Goblet

It was sunset—an image prevailed:
The sky like a goblet holding the light,
A man standing there with enormous thirst
As if the day-long draft of the sea failed,
The wine at the table could not appease—
I know these days one should not say such things.
The world is set on the hard stuff, and "the real"
Seldom chokes on itself in the bottle—
A glimpse, a divot of sunset, quite enough.
But I love these expansive views that hold
A magnum for the megalomaniac
Who still wishes the world had its world view,
That a thing so simple as a sunset
Could still spread an immense saturation,
That one could come here with all one's daydreams
And imbibe, mouth and throat like an hourglass,
Infilled with light and then turned again.
It is not that days on the beach do not
Leave blotches, sunburn, the feet cold as lapis—
One brings these offerings to libation:
The scar where the flying whisky bottle struck,
The blue mole that needs electrolysis,
The doubts, cross purposes, and dissensions,
The raised welts of a Weltanshauung—
It is that one clears with the spreading light:

A hint of vine leaves, a kind of hero's bowl,
The lips almost carmined with rapture,
A splash of gold on the old canvas shoes.
Somewhere hidden in us, I do believe,
There's a desire for acute sensation
That does not linger on some dubious point
But flares and flares in a fast-fading sky:
The power, the proposition without pose,
The heart finding the great hourglass imbued—
We could discuss it for hours and hours,
But rather let us stand, sore and sea-soaked,
And drink and drink until our rims are one.

Wild Oats

Perhaps it came down to that—the lover,
The lemon trees, a view of the blue sea,
And somewhere blowing in the wind wild oats
Like seed to keep you young forever.
It is something you must take from the air,
It makes the eyes smart, leaves musk in the nose—
All because she lies naked beside you
Like the warm subject for a work of art.

Therefore we practice these gestures over
And over in secret, the casting out
And the reining in, youth not being half
Long enough for the crop you have in mind:
The inseminated fact, the furrows
That open everywhere until the stone
On her hand looks like a swollen grain,
The citrine of parthenogenesis.

No doubt, you choose the jacaranda tree,
The purple blossoms and the amethyst,
The dark lady lying by a river.
Arrange the subject, and the seed will fall.
The water, perhaps, has turned dark as black grapes,
And you will feel fertile with fatality—

In a dark hall, the throes, a dangerous mood,
The old torn overcoat sagging with groats.

I can tell you that it never passes,
The performance before the fact that counts.
It is the only way: Expose yourself—
This is where the seed touched down, took root.
All of those mornings of the outflung hand,
And the curving and the swift reining in—
Stay out on night patrol if need be—Feel
And smell the wild oats blowing through the world.

Blue Dancers

In the midst of crises, the insolence of fortune and appetite,
One tends to summon something that moves freely on its own:
Dry your tears. There are blue dancers in a soft blue light.

Love has made you this once more a plaything and a fool:
Hot palms, hot feet, dry tongue, the parched lips of longing—
Apply the poultice of a picture, dancers in blue tulle.

I know it pulls away even from your magnifying glass,
Devolves into the very vortex you despise—
Drama is jealous of pictures, and pictures say: This, too, will pass.

What have we here?—The world withdrawn, the world is moving
    faster,
The day destroys philosophy as hard as you can tug the scene:
Blue clown, admit that you must be a dupe before you are a
    master.

I have these scumbled pictures on my hands—
One would think that I had dipped them in a vat of blue,
But, in fact, I have stacked them up against—how many days'
    demands?

It is a powerful sensuous surge, another taking over—
Master, tap your cane, tell them how and where to move:
Blue dancers educate the fool and elevate the lover.

The Pond

Do you remember those days we went fishing in the pond,
Wore cut-off jeans, no underwear,
Drank cola in the sun, and did not think that we must share
With anyone a having to ourselves the Great Beyond?

This is a focus filled with jeweled light—
We stripped, tanned beneath its magnifying glass,
Felt the prism in the blood, the rainbows pass,
Their colors, like a Dance of Seven Veils, unite.

For naked boys, the shimmering gauze—
I take some comfort that it comes to me so late
The most alive of us can lie in state
And break the rigid pattern of eternal laws.

I smile to see the old man in the mirror
As though he saw the pond in morning glow,
And knows in unforgotten places time is very slow,
Waits in grave attendance at the edges of an error.

An error with the most imposing truth in it—
A jeweled ring that dazzles on my finger
The rich belabored dance of those who linger
Yields as little to attendance as those edges still permit.

The Truss

Just that pad on a special belt—a touch
Of something firm, and a sea wall rises:
The blue, adored and feared, is held in check.
Still one shakes, shivers, spits out a bit of foam.
There is a blue rocking in your shoes,
An hallucinatory desire for puttees,
Their low, supportive signals to the truss,
Warning the pad to harden like sapphire.

128

Furthermore, you are advised not to lie
Languidly in a hammock's slumped canvas,
For all your strength will seem heavy and bagged.
It is being held, helped, upright that counts,
The exoskeletons of your legs chiding
The raised head to find the sacred river,
To answer the full sea with source-waters,
To have a hummock, a hill, for yourself.

There will be time for violets at your feet,
Indeed, low-slung hammocks that do not pinch,
A supple jewel holding a healed place,
But when that time will ever be, who knows?—
I hear old men mumbling of golden years,
And want to break off a headland for them.
Meanwhile, one gains, gathers a kind of youth,
Feeling these tremors of a tightening world.

The Premise

Hawk-shaped, the shadows of the diver fall
Into the way the pool argues out its blue.
The body, some do not know, can be a harsh thought too—
Consider, in larger terms, the weighted parachute's bolder
    universal.

An umbrella collapsed, a plummeting bird—
These are the facts of fall on which to trade.
One could set up a metaphysical racket with the aid
Of any two of these that mutually concurred.

I offer, however, a beaked shadow, the chute
Of an unknown body, quite merciless to ground.
But even here we range the world too wide, confound
The issue of the swimmer, half figment in a feathered suit.

Let us close in on fall, believe the pool
Which cleanses hawks and gives us man—
Surely we flicker in doubt, and no one can
Be sure he knows what went into the beautiful.

Last Word

It was as though the sea rose up and stuck
Out its blue tongue at him with the last word—
Was it a kind of lump sum of language,
Would it come crashing down on him at last?
Was he, in fact, the last of a lost tribe
Who had tried to face down the mammoth mouth?—
It was only one of those immensities
That loom some days in towering regard.

I must keep a civil tongue in my head
When the extravagant sunset insists
That a rapt plethora pervades the world,
A rich, pink wine pouring into the sea,
The blue lips engorged, engulfed, backing off—
You have seen that pulled and placid water
When the end of the day has had its way
And a gull floats like phlegm in the great throat.

Then the blue night comes on like a numen,
And you are asked for prayer and evensong:
No stepping back, feeling for the night latch
Though the sudden lamp looms like a loophole—
One thinks of warm thighs, the lodestone of love,
The retreat to a place where nothing matters:
Two people, jammed, lying by a wicket,
Speechless, counting on dawn to let them through.

The Cove

Was it a new or a remembered place—
Too calm to hold his life's rough history?—
His boat had lost its calligraphic power,
The placid water like a vast blue mirror
That swallowed all his spoken sentences.
Only the touch of glittering dragonfly
Flitted, here, there, across the stalled morning

As though punctuating a vacuous page.
Even the sun looked bald from spreading out
Its light, and the hazy, violet hills,
By contrast, looked mad, savage with dyed locks.
Of course, no litterbugs were on the beach,
No village and no steeples to push down—
Was it time to weigh anchor or reminisce?
A compulsive image kept coming back:
A girl in a canoe, the parasol,
His face tanned, his shoulders hard as topaz,
The incredible intaglio they cut,
The shape of a love-knot in the water,
A figure repeated on soft, inland grass—
As if the crotch always preceded the cross,
Her purse like a silk pouch, stretched out, crammed
With the makings of the bird of paradise,
His moist straw hat beside them like a nest.
Of course, one can throttle the manic fly,
And the story ends, the sun grown senile.
The savages have lost their appetite,
The flesh long marinated in the pot.
Only ants carry their wafers of the world
As if an enormous, brisk sense of wings
Had been grounded in their green desires—
Perhaps it is just the iridescent buzzing:
A fish leaps like a phallus from the water
And lands gasping, quivering in the boat,
Perhaps your loaded, lounging hand picks up
Luxuriant blue tattoos from the warm water
As if the sun were needling you again,
As though senility simmers, then sears—
I have had so many idle summers
With the last anchor hung between my thighs,
Words no more than wisps of smoke in the mouth,
Feeling the cove has come for me at last—
No inland foot, no shadow on the ants,
The purse rifled, the hat singed by a brushfire.
Perhaps it is nothing but pictorial surge—
I feel the topaz leaching from my arms,
And I study all my old incisions.
If she could read me like a book, it would
Be lurid with just this love of living—
So tell your children's children where the cove

Will lie, waiting well below the cross.
We go on inland, upward—there it is—
Save that lasting image for the very last,
But loll until you lavish in the sun,
And give your final kiss to what may be.

The Fox and I (1996)

I

The Pirogue

It was a humid tank town of the South,
Festering with flowers, plump girls, men in jeans.
Red, blue, trucks ruptured the silence now and then,
Rutting the hot mind with assignation.
The swamp nearby was a kind of relief:
Bears, alligators, frogs, and Spanish moss,
Varied, inevitable movements, vocalise
Of birds that do their mating dance for us.

One needs to watch the man in the pirogue:
Perhaps a prisoner on parole—who knows?—
Surely a rich mystery in a flat boat,
Totally at ease in the somnolence
As though the town had let him out to graze.
There is a kind of strange insolence here
As if we want a pariah of peace,
Someone out there with the skating dragonflies.

Behind the lush girls, blue men, this icon—
We can pile into the trucks, bring him back
Any time we want, a captive on call,
Loll and laugh at his stories of swamp life:
How the bear beat him to the honey tree,
The alligator's lust for his white legs,
The sensual stroking of the moss, the birds
With their sharp, thrilling tattoo on his heart.

Out there, still, the pirogue ready to drift—
When the men take the girls that night, they dream
Of the swamp by the bedside, the long pole
Prodding the bottom like a soft carpet.
You will not slide out of the world that way,
Young man, young girl. The hot towns deceive us.
Nothing if not both: the real, the backup—
The convict at the bottom of the lake.

African Afternoons

It was brilliant summer and the time for orange chiffon—
But you were tired of the woman, did not want to wrestle with her
    moods,
And did not care what she was taking off or putting on.

Some rich nerve connected with her was no longer being fed.
Yet here she was coming toward you, golden-haired, lucid, loosely
    draped,
As if, in the old way, by making love alive, to knock you dead.

Strategically placed, the orange lilies in a vase
Would give their muted, or more blaring, background music
While she decided what tempo and what action were demanded
    by this latter phase.

So hot and heady, it was like afternoon in Africa to you—
The lioness had hunted and you had fed and fed and fed,
A time for lying down beneath the trees with nothing thrilling left
    to do.

Ah, the stretching, the lolling, the letting-go—this time I pass—
You have absolutely lost your dark, mysterious sense of avatar:
Just wait until she rises, golden, burnished, from the tallest grass.

Don't ever think that, for the over-petted one, Africa is over—
Night comes on, the lilies drop their pollen, chiffon rustles,
And you are still the unfed cub who needs some practice as a lover.

The Tent

Purple clouds the color of bruises—
It was time to go in, nearly sundown.
The tent is the place for those whose dreams
Have never added up. Pitched on the earth,
Bare of pictures, a cot for you and me,
Folding camp chairs, some rations, knives, a gun—
Otherwise, nothing but us, unless we
Get lucky, make a culture of our breath.

Not that we had not tried it all before—
Down by the lily pond, our mouths were pressed
Together in the same lovestream. Duped
Or drugged? Too much logic or sentiment?
Even wildflowers were posed hypocrites,
The squirrel froze, scampered, but it could not roar—
The campout, meant to be African, vulgar,
Had brought us back to the incubator.

Why can't we undress at least in tattoos?—
Fire flickers beyond the flap of the tent;
After supper, the raw smell of burnt flesh,
Stars that have watched millions of sacrifices
Simmer down, ask for our encomium.
Before bed, we eat an actual apple
And think of the legends we have consumed:
Surely a core, rind, somewhere on the ground.

Did the lilies, meat, stars, work overnight?
Does the tent smell of regeneration?—
Is this what we mean by manic dreams:
Liebestod among the lilies, singed meat,
An imprecation to the old, clear stars?
I told you not to pack too much—to pitch
The tent at the right angle where the sun
At dawn spots the snake spitting diamonds.

Front Porch Glider

Shut your eyes and dream a gondola that goes and stays,
Tethered in one place and yet always slightly easing forth—
In summer, so we dream, at last the choice is two ways.

One feels hot, tired, wounded somewhere deeper than the brain—
Move a little outward on a rich, Venetian dream,
But not too far, too mad, enpurpled—the softest bump, and you
    are home again.

When the soul wants everything, what can equal such a ride?—
The rope that ties the gondola is made of silk and gold,
And with such infinite finesse—back and forth—calibrates the tide.

We will break free, no doubt, we cannot live forever on such
    braided tether,
But something on this sumptuous, dream-engorged, gilded
    afternoon
Tells us we have found a perfect lullaby for summer weather.

It takes some confidence, of course, a love of never being bored
To see the lavish, ducal buildings and never feel oppressed
As if the Grand Canal, confined, hugged close, were little better
    than fiord.

There is such a shimmer on the lilies, such a sense of water in the
    eyes:
From minimum to what we have of maximum, we oscillate—
The wounded hold the world a while to just this ebb and rise.

The Crop Duster

How could he psyche himself up one more time?
How could he spread his folded wings in awe?—
He could lie in sleep, his pajamas pupal,
His dreams the stuff of mashed cocoons,
The rapid eye movements a quivering

138

Of metamorphosis. But when he rose
And stripped, could he rely on the mirror
To reflect no figment of his folded state?

One may want all of the love in the world
And yet rise, naked, begging for fig leaves,
Long for the full, ecstatic flight and settle
For the dream of the earwig, the brain worm
That never can go glittering in the sun.
It will do no good to use ear drops
That drip on the pillow an insect's trail:
A live thing in the mind still wants to fly.

Somehow he ravishes among reflections,
And rises fully loaded in the sky.
We look up at him, crammed with our mixture,
As he goes back and forth, a mammoth moth—
The clouds of dust are almost orgasmic:
Is it health, horror? Is it happiness?
The day that follows has its miasmas:
We are the focus of the duster's swoon.

Flowering Judas, Later

The betrayer's tree is more beautiful
Than any other to those who have been
Betrayed. It is the late, ornate style,
One might say the grand, luxurious style,
Which ambiguities may revel in.
Who swung and thumped from the tree? Who was it?
We sway as we walk, empurpled, thick with style.
At the end of the lane, as in a mirror,
The tree stuns us with its suave accretions.
Must the world always remind us of ourselves,
Do we turn the corner, go down alleys,
Only to see the dense life waving there?
Old women in purple and gentlemen
With lavender ties find these boughs like arms
Embracing and returning them freely

To the wind. Time is more tolerant than we
Are wont to think, kinder even to traitors,
And we need not be so sure what we did.
There is an ample bench beneath this tree
For the enrichened ones where they drink wine
As spring wanes like a great bruise over them.
The women pull their purple stockings up,
The amethyst stickpins of the old men
Are like the eyes of Judas as they doze—
It can be sensed all around them, the stuff
They were and will not part with, and the wind
Cannot turn the heavy page without betrayal.

The Fox and I

When the fox has eaten his last peacock,
The shuddering, masticated iridescence,
I must look into myself for rainbows
As if I myself had eaten the bird,
A rinse of gold and purple in my mouth,
An intestinal flux of bright feather,
My rustling, dark hair gleaming with halo—
A man of my age is stuffed with farewells
As though the day had been stretched and broken,
Stretched and broken to an inward bleeding,
Hallucinations of the last peacock,
This quaking and quivering in my throat,
The crown going through the jewel-picking teeth—
I gulp, gasp, and recast a corona,
The aura of my life, in the hope something
Will light it like a gas ring, let it flare,
All of one's goodbyes in this spectral form.
Out in the fields I know the young are hunting
The fox, stuffed with their own iridescence,
In their blood-red coats and their great rich lusts,
The beautiful rush, the day still unbroken.
I go into the kitchen, light the stove
That glows like the scraps of cremated birds.
So the fox and I have eaten our fill—

I sit at the table, dreaming rainbows,
Mists of metaphors rising from a maw.

Amber

How long the great tree dripped for just one bead
Is anybody's guess—The odalisque
Would never know she wore its fossil tears,
Lying naked in an amber necklace—

A barrier reef of voluptuousness,
The beads snaking down between her large breasts,
Looking for eggs to hatch the basilisk,
The long lost lair of the lachrymose tree.

Perhaps there's a fly caught in the amber
Like a small winged cinder leached from the eye
As if pine trees wanted an irritant
To let down their feelings so in public.

Unquestionably one thinks of languid shores,
Nudes left in an almost denuded place
As though the tide beached this fabulous bulk,
Her buttocks stuck with the makings of beads.

Do not ever think that such clarity
Is really strained of the world's rich droppings.
The white nude herself is a full, dropped thing
As if the flesh-tree cried and she was born.

Therefore, let us be at home with fossils,
Watching her fondle them on her white breasts,
Raising a dolmen to the dead pine trees,
Lucid books piled together on a table,

Some scriptures for the day the buzz saw came.
I write this among the great fallen trees
Felled to make more room for a stifled house—
A woman on her knees, the unstrung amber.

It aroused the immeasurable, thick world in me,
How naked one lies to all creation—
I can imagine the huge trees weeping,
The brilliant shore pocked with resin, the nude.

Some day in the clear, cool, completed rooms
When the final fly has winked from the eye
And one is accustomed to all the flaws,
She will take out the long, superb necklace.

How do we live except to tell the beads,
The full string of the clear, strained circumstance?—
A light glows in the window, a bubble descending
Always and always to seers of tears.

Grasshopper

The small, dour, obdurate face is almost brutal—
One knows how he feels, how he got that way, one does indeed,
Every other little jump closed like a safety pin that just might stall.

This comes about, putting all the kinetic eggs in one basket.
If you cannot make the desired, expected leap,
You might as well be dead, *confrère,* littering the lawn with a little,
    stiff, viridian casket.

To anyone with the least determined, anxious, thrust,
You make a spiritual sound like the cricket in the crackerjack box,
So tinny, inconsequential, so sure to be left in the rain to rust.

Even flying is touched with tense, feverish intimations of chill.
What is flight indeed but a manic, forward, shivering in air?—
There is always the inevitable downward suction of space which
    has the stronger will.

So enter the summer porch in search of peace, a deeper and more
    inward look,
The still, protected, Pharaonic heart of green,
And land perhaps in totem on a much maligned and unread book.

142

acketed in green, the book acquires a colophon,
Tombed with the grasshopper in their little, hectic, springing
    effort—
A small, subdued, eternal pair lying in the sun.

Figures in a Compleat Season

The summer is replete when I conceive
The tall, dark woman with the bouffant hair
Sitting among huge watermelon slices
As though she intended a lush still life,
Small, controlled, but it got away from her,
Enlarging on its own a bright image-world—
There is a swamped sense of inundation
As if she must ride a curved, meat-filled ship
Or flood out on an ocean of pink juice.
This is what happens to these dark women
Who cut into a melon on the table,
Counting on little lipstick smears of color,
A blue dish if the patient really bleeds:
They are sorcerers of the arranged life,
Salome's sisters with their neat, quartered heads—
I used to see them on summer porches,
Their powerful hands passing out communion
To men with the unexposed white bellies,
The underside of fruit sun could not reach,
Hitching their suspenders and spitting seeds,
Sending out some black telegraphic code.
But the women never heard the SOS,
And only the child saw how the summer
Turned on them, threatened loose ships, a wild pink sea—
Now I can never smell a warm melon
In the sun without this protuberant sense
Of secret life beneath the picnic table—
I cling to the dark legs of sorcerers,
I plead with the pale side to turn over,
A swollen image wanting so much more.

Summer Night

It is a hard act to follow, the languorous man, the hammocked
    afternoons,
The watermelon and fruit ice—How does one summon at sunset
The white masked figure in the flowing pantaloons?

One lies at ease, a gentle air, one does not twist
Slowly in the wind, and is not caught, hung, enbagged:
It takes a vein of iron to be a supple hedonist.

The girl who brings you lemonade is part of this guipure—
There is a subtle strength in any net of pleasure:
One is tying tiny knots in it every moment we endure.

Endure an afternoon, that is, playing with all ends—
Someone is picking out a glamorous lace, strumming a guitar,
And you will make it into twilight with a little help from friends.

They want to ease you into moonlight and white mask,
From lush, redundant day, the poet of evening:
A little sorrow on the face of Pierrot is all they ask.

The white, white soul in you, and the shadows blue,
Some sadness, silver, in the iron-extended filigree:
You rise—that girl with a tear upon her face will dance with you.

II

The Break-Up

A master of sensual particulars
Will fear the hiatus above all else:
The thick sea developing a bald spot,
The palm trees dropping fronds like loose green hair,
The purple mountains grazing to nowhere,
One's own name growing vague on dry lips,
The lover's mole that threatens a black hole—
No wonder you hung her with false diamonds
Just to insure some kind of firmament,
Gasped in dismay when she wiped off her rouge—
Who did she think she was, killing impressions?—
A rainbow of desire streaked in cold cream.
It is the moment between when the tongue
Licks the sherbet, cannot remember the flavor,
Lying limp as a snake in the mouth's cave,
Having flicked back a great harlequin mound.
Stalactites do better, drip forever,
Dripping down their substance till it meets the cone.
You could choose many other signs, portents:
Fillings dropping as you eat the nougat,
The barrel's drouth when you drink your bottle,
A tulip shattering its ideal shape
As if someone overhead pulled a string.
I have even heard the suave pavane pause,
Having forgotten its sad peacock steps,
The eyes folded in a feathered barrow.

So we are brothers in the breach, but those
Who never ferret the gap in their teeth
And feel for the stone that lasts forever,
Who never undress, thinking of changes,
How can they live in yet another suit?—
I say this, having had so little luck
With glamorous elisions, seeing them part,
Having had the song pulled out of the ear,
Left with a kiss stencilled on a handkerchief,
The backhoe by the foot of the sherbet mound.
Still, shall we form a secret, sanguine cult
With just some stretched ecstasy as our dues?—
Gathering the sea's blue hairdo where it thins,
Impelled to record our postimpressions
When the heart rolls back upon itself,
Not minding the pink, pasted-on beauty spot,
The confetti that covers the black hole,
The pip in the paint, the patch on the tapis—
Lovers hugging the hint of lacuna
As if ruptures repaired rewind the song.

Return of the Native

The day that you decide that you have taken all you can
There is always one thing left to do:
Tap your heart and try to find the whereabouts of primal man.

He may prove to be, in part, a pleasant creature,
Somewhat stunted and repressed from long confinement
But still a sensuous little prince with hardly any comprehension of
    the future—

All trees, flowers, eating, mating, as though ingrown
In the best possible manner with the things of his desire:
A land where no one tears embroidery from the fabric on which it
    is richly sewn.

No hydrogen bombs, mind you, no fears. Nothing that is not Mine.
Then why is that pigmy running on the grassy cloth of gold

146

As though the embroiderer slipped his stitches and produced a
    roaring Lion?

Brilliant and ruthless he moves, an incendiary ball,
A full-dressed terror, if you will a kind of animal-bomb:
The mannikin was ill-advised about the nature of the crucial.

Tap on the heart and let the little creature in—
He slew the tawny King, stamped his fire into the grass,
And left us room upon the silk, strength and caution in the skein.

Petrified Forest

Sleeping on an arm, one has the feeling
That death is slowly taking over now
As if the night were necrophiliac—
One can envision a still, stiff forest
Caught in its last, flexible, windblown gesture.
So this is a dream-log, so one has sipped
And sipped from the night's stony nectar.
Therefore, one remembers the glorious, freakish sight
Of a bandaged finger, little soldier
That has somehow bivouacked on the pillow—
Gorgeous, free thoughts begin to flush again,
A pink grape in the dry throat is thawing,
The blue mouth is moist with forgotten lips,
But the arm clings and clings to its torpor,
And now when you rise, it is always mixed:
Foolish desires of bandages removed,
And illusions bleeding, cleansing the world—
The supple nude, hung with turquoise, bloodstone,
The skin touched with the sea's cyanosis.
One resolves never to sleep on an arm
Again—Foolish man, foolish child, the roll
Of sleep itself is contagious from the sea:
Even the fondled finger, the dried blood,
Is a kind of fossil of the future.
Therefore, think of turquoise, bloodstone, as bells,
The pause, the procession, as poetry.

A rose is lusting for you through its thorns—
Kiss the peach before it bronzes on the tree,
And let the swaddled soldier greet the dawn.

The Gold Tooth

In the vacuous soft paste of his white face
It was like the first piece of a mosaic,
Glowing with Byzantine nostalgia
As if someone made just a tiny start
And immediately ran out of metal,
The whole plump body an unfilled matrix—
Still, it seems to hold something together,
A square golden nail, a bolt through the head.

One tries to recapture brilliant figures
In the churches, the close-set, tamped down cubes,
The rough, cobbled texture of rhapsody,
But the smooth flesh keeps getting in the way:
Just this one indentation, this hard gap
In an otherwise vague interpretation?—
When the man puts his hand over his mouth,
A kind of avalanche settles on the soul.

Therefore one thinks of the Gold Rush fever,
The shoveling, digging at the old mountains,
The first, coarse, jagged spur of gold turned up,
How refined, reformed, it traveled to his mouth—
Stolid though he is, I would so grant him
The power of hinges he could swing the tooth,
Slowly glimmering outward in the dusk,
Like the smallest door to Eldorado.

The Minotaur's Brother

Some leaves drifted into the labyrinth—
It was autumn and the bull man was dead.
Did someone forget to feed him the maidens
Or, for some queer reason, the diet palled?
(In that dark artery anything could happen.)
Perhaps in the end he left them like tubers,
Not through mercy, but wanting them to sprout:
Everything begins, ends, in the gut of the world.
In any case, he had known all along
There was a brother, the lazy fumbler,
The one who was learning the visceral trade.
They worked two seamed halves of the labyrinth
Once they learned how long a spool it really was—
Just now the brother learns the elder cheated:
He had never switched sides, devoured a maiden,
Never known about the opening at one end
With flowers and a cleared place for love,
One girl at a time, taken, and let go—
What happened then, the brother wants to know—
All that subterfuge, freedom, all that lust
While he mined the close backside of the world?
Who was his famous brother after all?—
One thing he found where the wall's skin was hard,
A drawing done with blood and burnt stick,
The minotaur grazing on beds of poppies,
Red and black, colors of the underground.
Someone else now buried in the other end,
The brother steps out into the autumn light,
Letting the elder's loss shake down like dust.
It was so good to share at last, to know
He had this brother captured in the dark,
An autumn knowledge perhaps, but warm, so warm,
The vein would sprout with maidens in the spring—
He throbs openly at the end of things,
His long fingered hand, gold as a dahlia,
Crawling with dying bees, clutches the sun.

Zombie

Was it the taste of her lips, the cocktails,
Or the slow, acrid savor of the world?
Between half-closed eyes, the blue of the sea
Was like a long knife laid across his brain—
Sunrise could not lift his lids, nor sunset
Pull him back down again into the grave.
He could faintly remember when the doors
Of sex closed, even the labia of books.
Someone was feeding him poison, but how,
When, where?—a dead-fish smell on his sleek skin.
Some might say he had gone crazy, his mouth
Filled with the gray pearls of imprecision,
Unchewable corundum of the rich day
Into which he had bitten too lushly.
Nude women called him like a locked lighthouse,
Rejection, seduction, the old two-way pull—
Was it really all those mixed drinks, those loves,
The rum and the rumor going in and down?—
Breathing out that jewel-mist, the fine spray
Of his steeped, rank, world intoxication?—
I toy with these notions as I sit down
To write my latest love, a hot ruby
Rising in my gut, my heart on a hill,
The pores rinsing out the old clogged poison.
Can I say at last what I could not say
When I was laid in the box, silvered, soldered?—
I stir the zombie with a long straw, sip
And sip as though I milked pigmy entrails.
Is it better, richly sodden but small,
Or, coming back, to call the tribe to see
If they have grown more subtle, delicate?
Ah, those letters never sent!—the strange rush
When you lift the eyelids of a dreaming man.
I am glad of the awning's dark visor
Where we sit beneath the cap of caution,
The mixed blood of the drinks, your glowing bracelets
Which answer hillside signals on a lower plane.
The book of poetry, spattered with fruit juice,
Echoes our long, visceral entanglements—
Is it late enough, light enough, to read?

150

Extremadura

In Extremadura I could find my lair
Among wild lavender, black storks, vultures, wolves, cork oaks—
There must be a place for secret, saturated passion somewhere.

Absolute desire is hardly countenanced anymore:
The wish to run with the wolf, fly with the stork, roll in lavender—
We take the easy epicarp, and never find the core.

There is lavender in perfume, potpourri, and sachet,
But when the body thrashes out the wild, essential attar,
The scent will go beneath the skin to stay.

I have memories of the white enfabled stork
Whispering that life must stretch on through sun and shade, light
     and dark,
And here the final, imperious black twin lights upon the cork.

One wants of course, forever, all the seasons of the Word,
Not distracted from each exclusionary focus, but clear,
     powerful,
Slow, deep, high, low, the transhumance, the cautious herd.

In Extremadura, I would at last release the brook—
One can be lavish when the heart has known the hardness and the
     drouth:
Just this morning I could hear the murmuring and the rustling in
     some half-completed book.

III

The Cable

It had come to him out of nowhere—the thought
Of the cable, how his own blue-veined arm
Might string him up, a twist of the sky's color,
This longing to be heavy with heaven—
He remembered his lover' long, bright mane,
How she might hang beside him, hair-strung,
Twisting in ecstasy from a gold rope
As if his free hand turned her to a pitch.
Perhaps deep down in love we deal in strands,
The plaited emotions looking for tension,
Putting clamps on the heart to make it swell,
Letting out the flow from a tumid spool.
Nerves run through the body like filaments
Of silver—A deep kiss pulls on the line
And the whole trellis shivers compliance—
Who is that camoufleur working the crane,
Dangling the hook like a shepherd of the sky,
Wanting the raised arm and the knot of hair?
These projections give us philosophy—
Your first, warm smile alerts the puppet:
I dance to the tips of your deft fingers,
Turn in a glow and set you in motion;
Someone is cranking the coil on your head.
Ah, the pirouette, at last, in blue space!—
We close in a dream of flying angels,
So blue, so gold, a dangling human cord.

152

We settle entwined—Calypso dancers
Give us an island full of vines and fruit.
Is it to be half-hung standing, just so,
That we beg the air itself for blended being?

Exaltation of an Aesthete

Let us review the sensuous, intricate woman sitting on her porch—
No one but I, perhaps, would know how she burns in her paradise,
That this cool woman in her beautiful dress is something of a
    human torch.

Her garden is meticulous, her low-cut dress without a crease—
She has been put into a world she truly wants and loves,
Striking the eye with that clear force, a declamation of Matisse.

And yet this woman lives, so I am told by those who do not like her
    pure Gestalt,
In earthquake country, right on the mystic, meandering line,
The good side pulling at the bad in simulation of a fault.

Through some coarse, abrupt, unaccountable slippage of desire,
The exquisite house she lives in, the very dress she wears,
On the most lucid day of all, will suddenly catch fire.

I am told more than this, partly believe it, and yet
I will dream with her all of a long, lucent summer's day
Above the lines of instability that part without a safety net.

I do not mind the latency, the subtle lust for doom—
I even have a vision: whirling down together in a brilliant glow,
Two torches fused when both our sides would make the world a
    single tumbling room.

Studbook

When his eye-to-eye control had lapsed,
The woman's face pulled like a postage stamp,
The sea withdrew its constant blue claque,
Even the fountain ached in its bladder,
And roses held back their hot shriveled lips.
So the man learned one of life's basic stories—
She is off somewhere redoing her makeup,
The sea is redirecting its applause.

Not to speak of the rose's repulsion,
That one's own fountain cannot make water—
One silvers then, one seeps with sensation,
Meaning too slight, without sticking power,
The plump finger sweating its *cire perdue,*
A ring, but no soft breast for sealing wax.
It is then you begin to consider impressions,
How little you can list in the studbook.

She does come back, the fresh, redrawn beauty,
The sea promises a standing ovation,
The fountain lavishes its lyric lies—
But cold shoulders last longer than warm, the kiss
Keeps the power of the wet postage stamp,
The rose pouts with its louche, go-go manners—
Therefore read, read from your book to the sea.
It could be generous if you call its bluff.

The Jack

It had been a day of lifted burdens:
The fallen fruit and the stumbled woman.
Her beads spreading everywhere, large as grapes,
Her gold chain sprawled, a slackened lifeline,
As if you failed her in some steep ascent.
A whiff of some missed cave in her armpits,
The blood-smears of lipstick on the green carpet.

154

It will take more than skill at fixing
Flat tires, propping up the shed,
Lifting large objects to the highest shelf.
Her rings have spikes in them, her pull lethal,
The debris both heavy and delicate.
The pendant may slide in between her breasts—
A stretched girdle and pop goes the weasel.
One might lie down, of course, languish a bit,
Daydream in the dazed and lush deshabille,
Ponder the soft roll of the ripe peaches:
A rest from hours pumping in the sun,
The lust for odalisques one overlooked,
A sortie into shorts and stocking feet—
Nevertheless, it is time to pick up the grapes
That bruise the arches as you plush for wine.
It might be easier to tilt the floor,
Let everything but love slide down the slope,
The rumble of rings, the fruit in riprap,
Then the received woman in a raised kiss.
I have worked my arm sore in such service
Among summer dreams of fallen women,
Come from the hot road to the cool cascade,
Splattered and blinded with rushed diamonds,
And felt the wall of desire curve my way.
Picked up, look how refreshed she always is—
I live like Atlas bathed in splashing tears.

La Vie en Rose

The man who was the man who did not want to blunder
Looked over the field, it was a field of roses,
Thinking how good that he arrived, no longer living there, down
    under.

He had been a bit of a wild man in his not so palmy days,
An aboriginal of all life's doubts, hates, fears—
How had he come at last to these more dulcet ways?

Was it when the woman, the mythical woman, came to the mouth
  of the cave,
Liked what she saw, and threw him a rose,
That he had his first presentiment of how to behave?

Many roses thrown and, then, many, many rose-soft kisses—
It takes a while to build the notion of a view
Which overlooks the place where bliss is.

Then there it is, the ravishing, long, memorial garden—
No doubt, from time to time, something aboriginal shudders in the
  shadows,
The woman of the roses has a touch that promises to harden.

I know, having felt the warmest love go statuesque:
After the rain of roses, a little marble in the kiss—
Of all the things the wild man did, this was the greatest risk.

Hang Gliding

The huge rocks, the blue sea, and the lovers
Lying entwined, their heartbeats synchronized,
So it seemed, in an enclave of desire—
The rocks for fortitude, the sinecure
Of the sea, the mounting voluptuousness,
A pallet of sand like powdered topaz.
You get the picture, or, of course, you don't.
You can say to yourself, No, not my thing—
Somewhere, perhaps another low-swung scene:
Crumpled lovers, another persuasion,
I do not quarrel with unslung heroes.
But for now, for me, this rhythm of rafters
As if I hang in a picture-hammock,
Up high, looking down on lovers, the sea:
A rocking cocoon, open to air and light,
The mimetic cavalcade of clouds,
Deliciously lined with phoenix feathers.
Oh, to stretch out in oneself a moment,
Taking up all the slack in happiness:

Scoop up the supple people on the beach,
The hand an alcove of miniatures—
This luxury, this visual limbering up.
So wonderful to feel both heavy, light,
The slung grab bag of grace and gravity,
Back and forth, the arm hung down to trawl
The long, lazy sprawl of life for images.

IV

Chuck Wagon

Sometimes far up in the mountains or on the open plain
One has a steeped, concentrated sense of life:
We have paused for an afternoon, the night, and will not come
    again.

We have pitched camp, built fires, a commonality of wills—
It seems almost mystic to be here, not somewhere else:
The scent of men and animals, smoke and sizzling bacon in the
    nostrils.

One can dream back to bagnio, barrio, as if we were another race—
How they came to be where they were, their stuff and steam:
Just across the mountain, the signal fires report another place.

The earth knits up its mountains, releases plains at rest—
There's meat, fried potatoes, coffee round the wagon
For the rawboned husband, weathered wife and child at breast.

Here a concept is thrown down, goes up to God in smoke
    unfurled—
It may be nothing more than where we are in these tectonics:
Across the continents, the houri in the harem also smells the world.

If the earth, loosening, squeezing us together, silk shoe, bare foot,
    and boot,
Kneads a kind of cabalistic text no one can altogether read,

Does the rattler on the ground remember—regret, rejoice—that
    once it offered us strange fruit?

The Crank

His veins, so he thought, were filled with blue blood,
He had some well-concealed gold in his teeth,
And a large diamond on his finger—
No wonder the day would not turn over.

Maybe his love had put knockout drops
In his drink when he came on much too strong,
The hangover just the weight, remembrance,
Of all things desired and never achieved.

What did she want then—cold feet at climax,
To tie off the whirlwind in a condom
And shunt the shower of galactic spread?—
Indeed he had rolled off the planet then.

But not clever enough to have said this
Then and there, to have told her all extremes
Are like adventures born of loneliness—
The wit one remembers on the way home.

Well, then, old noises can and must be made,
The creaking bed, the buzz of the razor;
Orange juice can be poured down like yellow oil,
Marmalade in the jar looks thick as grease.

One would like a wrangler in the bedroom,
Herding up these rebellious emotions,
Driving them out to pasture in bright light,
But that image is heavily in hock.

I remember the old cars, how the men
Turned the crank as if awakening the world,
The girl in the flowered hat like Eden:
She did not mind the smudges on his hands.

159

What a maelstrom we live in—how it stalls!—
It takes some doing to restart the day:
The dagger in her eyes a shaft? And then—
All those vibrations of supposed content.

Wild Horses in the Snow

They seem to want to tell the earth something that they know,
Violent, hemorrhagic, rearing up into the air, stamping the frozen
    grass,
Snorting, running passionately back and forth across the snow.

They exude a strong scent of sweat and steaming ordure
As if the powerful, hemostatic, cold should understand
That it is only transiently pristine, basically impure.

We rub our ruddy hands together, stamp the ground,
Blow white, susurrant, breath into the brilliant air,
Inordinately sure and proud of the fact that we abound.

The horses thump their message on the white lead tympanum—
We ride out to see them, get down from their more gentled
    brothers
As if to press our own brusque rhythm on the roughly trampled
    drum.

We go home, our houses steam with this rubescent heat:
We thaw like hairy roses in our baths, embanked in bed,
And hardly a man jack of us will dream of ultimate defeat.

Nor will wake to it. For we shall breed as long as there is any sun—
We send this thunderous message into earth as horses do—
Who wants, indeed, to brook the faintest doubt about the thermal
    force of passion?

Stalactite

The decision is psychological—
The slow dripping or the slow building up.
The cave looks like the mouth of a monster
With horrendous teeth, but one whose huge jaw
Is locked on open. This lets the mind come
In, wait, and contemplate its choices.
I seem to prefer the drop suspended
Rather than settling on the reaching cone.

A little like that pause before you speak
As if it gathered from a sense of style
Into long, stretched, judicious savoring.
There are even moments when the stylus
Holds and does not wish to commit itself—
Much as the pen hovers, and there, far off,
The extravagant sea must be content
That some at least are not wastrels of blue.

But in your mouth itself, these stalactites:
The silent "Ah" before awesome moments,
Utterance itself finally so avid.
So if I do not favor stalagmites
Quite as much, believe, I, too, am a wastrel
Of blue, and must recant to solid ground,
The opposition, at last, spurious—
The long bite dreams and dreams, comes down to chew.

Sunset Casino

The dice had been dipped in blood, but the red
Stuck only to the dots, otherwise white,
Bone-white, as if carved from his own body.
Thus the Blue Man plays out another day,
Jangling his collection of set red eyes
In his pocket—one more play on the table.
If he had bathed them in the sea,

Would they have come up blue, world-weary, washed-out?
Rubbed, abraded against his bronze body?
But they would not cry their eyes out, nor give
Up their hard insinuations of the bone.
How much comfort can you get from gestures?—
The throw that says life is only a bet,
That you were born with red eyes, bone pieces—
The black ones come later, the funerals
When little tombstones flash their foolish numbers.
Therefore, this is a young man's game, the son
Of the sea, the Blue Man who plays to win.
When he comes home, lays down his briefcase,
He feels it heavy with a surplus bronze,
His testicles warm in their strange balance
Hung down, it would seem, from a golden heart,
The red rub-off in his glowing pockets.
A quiet glass of wine roars of the waves,
The risk of a kiss turns purple on the mouth
As though love were a throw in the face of fate.
If real blood is needed, perhaps the brooch,
The pin prick's little intimate stabbing:
The heavy man leans to his homecoming.
And yet the gross winnings are winsome:
Dice on the night table fixed in a grin,
Only the slight grimace of blue beads,
The flung clothes, the flight of another day.
I give you these blue people in barter:
Use all of your gifts for crisis control,
Tell me your dice are eyed with diamond
On a gleaming background of hard, red bone—
I hoard up a heap of discarded things:
All I want is the chance of a lifetime.

The Great Train Robbery

The man was not without considerable force,
But kept his vitality in boxes
Much as he did his cuff links and rings—
Down deep, in fact, a rich, bedizened man.

But life and energy are not ornament
Though it accents a flowing, throbbing drive—
Even the freest savage wants a necklace
As if the glamorous skin needs bridling,
The strong horse in the heart, a hackamore.
We want the powerful, put-together thing:
The athlete dripping the jewels of his sweat,
The towel an easy halter round his neck
As he lords it in the locker room a bit
And lets a golden haze into the world.
Therefore, we do not mind being tagged
Somewhat—French-cuffed shirt and tiger's eye—
We like a woman who sweeps into a room
As if she picked up her adornments like lint,
The whole shimmer a symbiotic thing.
Naked at night, she will command the box
Not to take too much glory to itself
Even though the bracelets lie warm for hours.
Someone much like her will find her lying
In a pool of glitter, shorn but not shriven:
No remorse, excuses, the lids tight-lipped.
They will carry them out one day—those boxes—
Finger a while the residual wonder,
A stud against a great starred necklace,
Listen for the music and lost movement
As if those who have held up and robbed a train
Regret the powerful, sleek rushing through the dark.

Snow on the Mountain

He looked white, oh, so white, cold, remote, in many eyes,
But thought that he contained something viscid, red,
That, without much provocation, would, with not much notice,
     rise.

What would it take—a lush hibiscus held to cheeks
To show them how subterranean, in fact, he was?—
A curling of the lips like smoke escaping when he speaks?

They only see his high and snow-clad Fujiyama look
And think he cools the brilliant sunrise and the fiery sunset down
Just as any child might see the man as mountain in a book.

I must admit I am that child as well: the tinted glaze,
The touch of an hibiscus brush, the glowing and cosmetic wash—
Does very little to suggest what, if anything, it overlays.

So down in the valley—the coolie hat, the rich kimono?—
We think we have the simple and the very complicated art:
In my brown skin and your embroidered silk about the world we
    go.

We know, we know, we know—God helps us through
When the tropics make their move, the huge hibiscus flower, the
    dust, the smoke,
And we must be the ones who saw the face, the mountain, when
    they blew.

V

Antinomies for Vulcan

Put a bronze nude in a room that is red,
Red walls, red rug, carnations on a table,
So that it says to anyone too white of mind: Drop dead.

Nevertheless, the nude is in control—
If the room could move, it would turn around it like an axle:
Someone put the passion of his life in it, the soul,

As if to say I coach and counteract the blood.
She was white, the model, gloriously milky white:
The favors and flavors of her body were offered up like food.

It was a bold thing: instead of marble, go for bronze—
All of that red and lissom white might have curdled
Without the shimmering resonance of a gong sounded by a bonze.

Not a mood, a style, for every day and every hand—
Sometimes a blue room, a small, gold, glowing statuette:
A needle taken from a haystack when fire moved across the land.

The storm, perhaps, blew out, blew in, those walls glazed by fire:
Cire perdue—the bronze is done, the axle turns—
Drop dead, and live, a voice contends, from the center of desire.

The Dervish

The man was sitting in a gilded chair
Looking at the leaves, the fine chair a dream,
Of course, the desire to equal, live
Up to the tapestries of golden autumn.

This is the kind of man who can take ship
On a bucentaur, thinking of Venice,
And put a bridle on Bucephalus
When someone else's sleek horse rushes by.

You may want to hit him with a cleaver:
Look, you want too much—the leaf but not the chair—
The last trip down the canal so long ago,
Only a ghost with a bit between his teeth.

You draw up your chair and I draw mine,
A little conference on continuum:
It looks like shooting weather through the window,
Your clay pigeons and my golden pheasants.

Then I have the most violent desire
To turn these mentalities in a swirl—
Leaves, chairs, tapestries, men and guns
As if autumn wants just such mash for malt.

We smoke, talk a while and then, in fact, go
Out to the terrace to drink our lager:
I will give you the handsome, snaffled horse,
If you will let the sumptuous barge float by.

Something suggests a clamp—two men like Janus,
But then the light falls only on one face,
And the full, turning motion throbs again,
Perhaps just one body used as blender.

I am left with the window and the golden chair—
But, nevertheless, an excellent place,
Believe me, as the wind turns the falling leaves
Like the spumed dasher someone gave the Doge.

166

La Loge

Have you seen that painting of Bonnard, men and women in an
    opera box
As if they bolstered Art in being what they are,
And bolstered life itself against too many shocks?

The men in formal dress, with opera glasses,
The women in exquisite gowns, headbands, and necklaces—
They seem to say that, so accoutered, they confront whatever
    passes.

In this case color and décor, the lyric passion on the stage—
The women have seen it all, heard it all before,
The glasses dangle from the hand as if the men did not need to
    magnify that page.

There are no children here, the parents form a richly figured wall,
A fortress of the heart which they have lurked behind themselves
Until the forefront summoned them with one command: never let
    it fall.

It will, of course, they know it, you know it, and so do I—
The music stabs and soothes, stabs and soothes, and stabs again:
Just so, they know they live and swoon, live and swoon, live and
    die.

I see the painting, hear the music, exposed to double-glow,
Recall the laughter of my parents, friends, as they built their
    screen—
The dancing, wine, and wizardry—and know it was not time for
    me to know.

The Cave Painting

The painting cries these days, and one expects
The tears to color the pale, upturned face
As if one were a stalagmite growing—

Even when yearning stacks up its capital
We cannot be as columnar as we should:
One girl drops the sludge of a black pocketbook,
A man in glasses, poor subterranean fish,
Waits for the wave that receded long ago.

We bring our metamorphoses inside—
A child screams like a savage sacrificed,
A woman pulls at the noose of long beads—
One imagines the wind of the desert,
Drying mould, clarifying the picture,
The black lines still warm from the long, charred pole.
Just be pure as the air for a moment,
The vegetable stains will look fresh as lipstick.

Now feel the stags and bison shake the earth,
See how the antlers leap toward the tremor;
Remember cement trucks warning the building,
Moving beyond reach the thunder of life!—
Say what you will—we raid the quietus,
Break into, break open, every essence,
The egg of a marigold for yellow,
The juice of a fruit to rouge the running loins.

Lie down beneath those pounding feet at night
As if they ground and fixed the colors on your skin—
Light as a canvas and closed as a stone
Before we lost our courage and our love.

Harlequin Head

You do not come easily to these changes,
The blue man looking for his Rose Period,
Kissing the peonies in the evening light—
They swab the face with medicinal perfume
And leave a white oval on your shoulders,
The eyes still there, ghostly touches of blue.
You break a few, swing them like censers
Through the garden, disinfecting the world,

Feeling now some faint rouge upon the cheek
As if slowly cured by that pale, pink smoke—
You have seen new ham hanging from the rafters,
How the color deepens in the smokehouse—
Right side up, drift in the peonies,
Let the hook of the hand lift up the head.
Dear heart, you are here for curing, blue meat,
Pink meat, perhaps the gangrenous future.
I have seen the bluest faces turn pink
Merely touching their lips to peonies,
The washed-out oval, warming, winking
As if blue eyes could run tears of blood.
Somewhere in our deep and eccentric love,
We marry all of this, the two figures,
Brilliantly translucent, posed in stained glass.
But for now, somewhat opaque, the pink smoke
In the garden, intermittently lucid,
Must let the lost brothers live by their moods—
I take the blue head back from the bruised world,
It smells of peonies, choked, choked indeed,
As if smoke rose too thick against the glass—
I do not mind if you should see my face
Peering at you from these life-illusions.

The Naked Truth

In the twilight filled with late, late roses,
Camellias, sasanquas, not yet taken by the frost,
I wonder what order, and disorder, the coming night imposes.

All afternoon on the sunporch I sat naked in the sun,
Thinking of things composed, imposed, myself a kind of flower,
Late, late, but not yet overblown, irremediably done.

The night, of course, will have a place for me:
Order, disorder—the huge, hybrid cosmic plan—
I remember the shining youth standing by a brilliant sea,

Also naked, feeling like some growth, some product of the water—
Ah, that blue, blue garden of long ago,
Promising to be fertile for all my dreams no matter,

No matter what. Now this floral matrix and the mellow tan:
I could drown heavily, if I want to, in accumulated dreams
Without much more accomplished, perhaps, than that a boy
    became a man.

The night so full. So fulsome?—how should one behave?—
I sit among flowers, naked, summon the glamorous early sea,
And lift one gilded arm above that blue, that dark, oncoming wave.

The Language Student

It is like touching the warm, clothed nipple
And the whole woman will shiver naked—
Nothing else but one more push—mood music,
And the world is incomparable spasm.
Since all is not sex and satisfaction,
I would advise: Line yourself with wonders
That lift, surge, and soar at the slightest touch:
A fallen leaf launches a golden barge,
A rising tear encapsulates a lake,
The lady's dropped ring hoarding the sea—
Under all hands this wide drift of life.
Of course, you sometimes come down hard, too hard,
And the nipple craters beneath the blow,
A tear spreads a spatula of grief,
And the blue light in the ring is seething—
When I come up from the pool and read
The language of gooseflesh, I, too, would be
Pressed for fine-tuning, and look for the hand.
I could be turned, in ardor, to a man
Of gold, smoothed down like a rough manuscript—
An eye on my chest will quake with papules:
A code raised on the surface of the tongue.

170

Untitled Picture

Now you have nothing left to dream—
That last camel with his eyes like roses
Left the canvas into a world which radically incloses
Things you cannot quite contain within an artful scheme.

Or can you? Call him back, the flowered camel,
And like a brigand riding him with rhyme
Make the blinkered beast commit the crime
Of making us believe a rose-eyed mammal.

There will be those who call for dung
In so much reverence for the steamed rosette
That half will hate the thought and half forget,
The fierce ride over, you fed him violets on the tongue.

I do not mean: Take one, I take the other end:
What comes from asses, comes from asses—
But when a camel wearing roses like sunglasses
Comes home, the sheerest edges of the dream extend.

The Haystack in the Needle

You went too long into the depth of things,
Now you were searching for the end of it,
The point pushed, then pitched into the unknown,
The dark brown mesh of meaning closing round,
An arm shriveled to a thread and then snapped—
The mind had called that much upon extension,
The needle lost for good in the haystack,
A vagrant, unintended, foreign body.

But you kept groping the fibrous network—
Here a cache of seed, there a tangled mass,
Palpating a tumor in disguise.
Illicit doctor without license,
Or a sad addict burning for a fix,

Ready to suffocate among the hay—
A small, tense blade of radium somewhere:
You must be cured forever of a concept.

Then the sudden prick, the bleeding finger:
The warm blood flushes as you push again,
An inflamed, swollen feeling in the steel,
The dominance, the daring, the breaking through,
A hemorrhage of poppies, a Monet field—
The pocketed needle, the looking back,
Under the thatch, the radiant structure:
It holds. You only dreamed you blew your stack.

Quizzical Bequest

Love seemed to have eluded us, and fame, so near, was out of
    reach,
But there on the white, white plate with a sharp knife beside it,
Looking up indubitably like an eye of reproach, the peach.

It spoke of fullness, richness, the surface of health, the pit—
This large, disembodied eye with its vibrations of reproachful
    vision—
It had seen sunlight, shadow, it seemed to say, registering all of it.

Where can be found a better position in life than hanging on a tree
Until someone rather blind should come along and want a
    fabulous visual aid,
A steady golden eye and yet a little red with so much there to see.

So must the wanderer at once decide, devise,
Forthright, to take the peach into the house, put it on a plate,
The master of the fatal, shining knife, a cannibal of eyes.

I like this wanderer who stares down at the plate but does not stare
    too long,

Whose own eyes, beginning to work, send out their subtle, tense commands,
A kind of aristocrat of how one feeds and keeps the senses strong.

So much for love and fame to which one always reaches—
One must appreciate them the more than one is ever appreciated:
I give you my eyes if you will, oh wanderer, eat them with peaches.

VI

Foil

The man in the white fencing suit looks at
A closed dictionary on the table,
En garde for the stifled, cautious word;
He is tense, alert, one knee bent for combat.
A flick of the buttoned foil will open
The book without tearing the secret page;
The magnifying glass's cloudy mouth
Takes up the matter from the cautious steel.

Have you not been poised with a point of view
And found language stiff as a fine-toothed comb,
Reached out for the suave exaggerator,
And seen a single word press up its belly
Holding a whole bag of blind intestines,
Or promising at least some heavyweight,
A fob in love with the touch of the sword,
Caution aside, the deep insinuation?

Touché. This is a very strange room indeed:
The fencer, the foil, the fat, dull book,
A glass mouth suddenly clearing its throat,
The buff of language exposing itself,
Keeping itself to itself for so long—
Only little pricks when the wan eye
Goes over it, hardly ruffling the nap
The well-cushioned text left unstigmatized.

174

Introduce at least the smooth bellied Fig,
Under the magnifier like a harem figure
Dancing in the dictionary till dawn.
It is, of course, both rich, irresolute—
You will see nothing but a close reader
In the room, an enlarger in secret,
But he plunges, plunges up to the hilt,
The pick of the harem naked on his foil.

The Liaison

Stepping out of the novel, I see a man
Somewhat like myself, yet changed, utterly changed—
Is it possible at all the novel turned on me? I ran?

Ran back to look at things so violent and grave,
Running up the hill, the blue man, the cliff, the sea:
A kind of standing bookmark in between those pages and the
    world that I would save.

I have stood so long indeed between the world and art,
Stepping in, stepping out, a kind of flattened icon:
Have you seen me on the cliff, between the pages, not knowing
    when to stop or start?

Not just the sea—the woman calls me to her side:
Why have I been gone so long and when and where?—
For any use I had to her I might have died.

Her glamorous face, her silk and pearls—I step back into those
    pages—
There are some still left and I their cutting edge:
She is right—I have not thought of her for ages.

Still, sitting in her bed having tea, Venus in her foam
Of pillows, she will not let me stay unpaged, blue and lonely on the
    hill—
She takes me out, I read her straight into the book and we are
    home.

Metronome

The late romantic masochist who thinks
That the core of life is always low life
Will not like the metronome, and indeed
It looks a little like an opened tomb,
One with a wagging tongue talking to time,
Shaped like a smooth Egyptian pyramid:
A throwback, a minuscule of history,
Until it stands guard on a piano.

The inverted pendulum has deep roots,
Exploring two sides of a confinement:
Never talking out of the side of its mouth,
The sliding weight adjusting its rhythm,
The monotony scored by the music.
And that may be truly the madcap thing,
Magniloquence pouring out of measure:
The dancing master tapping with his cane.

A little psychodrama is going on—
Leave the room, and just the cackling remains:
Silence is all, the cold stars, the cosmic night.
Nevertheless, the music of the spheres,
If we could ever get there, hear that deep—
Meanwhile, God gives us these toys on earth,
A rapt figure pouncing on a keyboard.

Sometimes a broken string, a finger sprained—
The metronome's Egyptian memories
Include the final pause, the end of time,
The pharaoh lying in a golden mask.
But whenever a shaft of sunlight spears
The tomb, the piano's odd sarcophagus,
Music still searches for a plundered throne,
Incognito, a chair upon a stage.

Blowgun

Looking at the rose, the prick of color,
He felt he had been struck by a blowgun,
Or as if the rich rose itself shot
Its thorns, a quiver of tiny arrows.

But you would not, of course, have seen him wince—
Better the savage not startled too soon,
Even though you see the headdress gleaming in the leaves,
Poised with the long pipe at his painted lips.

The sting, and then the long, sunken shiver—
The neural efflorescence, the blood called up
From its far counties, running in quick swales
As if to swamp round the ecstatic wound.

Somewhere in town a man with a blowtorch,
In his way, increases the intensity—
Something must be gotten into, in through,
A soft heart in the hardest material.

He would say that he has it all in hand,
But that struck Adonis in the garden,
Trailed forever by his own bright savage,
Gives on and on where the sharp point strikes in.

When steel burns through, indeed a kind of rose—
A lovely flare never to be discounted,
And a quiet, deep sleep while the berms of blood
Carry sensation to the open sea.

Still, in the morning one will resubmit,
Like Saint Sebastian, a beau ideal,
Some unsuspected mark for these roses,
Some small, fresh target for the brilliant eye.

It is common practice among lovers
To pluck out the dead arrows each evening,
A kind of good grooming without grievance:
Next time, next time, those swift shafts in a hail.

Not to be struck down dead by anything
But to find that relations of ravishment
Would one day make of the mouth a blowhole:
Ah, ah, so this—*that rose, that rose, that rose!*

Afternoon in a Yellow Room

Too much of anything requires a mix—
She knows her skin is white, and chose a yellow room:
That is, she stirred it in, in several shades, with different sticks.

Walls were white with lemon yellow borders,
Curtains yellow silk, some yellow chairs matted with white straw:
The painter, here and there, gave subtle orders.

It will not last, of course. Nothing does beneath the sun—
It will go shabby, bilious, rancid, out of style,
All of that beauty gone with the dandelion.

All of this she knows, looks in the mirror, predicts her fall:
The lines, the creases, gray as the fragile puff left on the flower's
    stem—
So she must be in love, or not at all, with things ephemeral.

The yellow clothes that lie in hostage to the moths—
Someone will come some day, a brisk, belated buyer,
To mock, misunderstand, the faded yellow humps beneath the
    dust cloths—

Not feeling palpitations, the joyousness of tint and tone,
The calculations, calibrations, spent on passing things,
Thinking that eternity is only found in stone.

The Bugler

All summer I reworked the image:
A well-wrought swimmer in a golden pose,
The tanned skin creamy and still unblemished
As if rolled daily in sunflower petals,
After the blue pool, the rich, whole-milk bath,
A private chemistry of preservation—
Someone, somewhere else, working his own mold:
One hopes for a heaven of ideal shapes.

It is incredible that the first brown leaf,
So early, could also be so earthly
As though lichens laid hands on our shoulders
Where the dead petals leave their decals,
The streams of old milk dried like white scars—
At this moment, sir, your strict attention,
As if reveille rushed to our rescue,
And you remove the idol from the fire.

Not to sit in total isolation,
One's own civilization just a dream—
Exit forever the idealist's exotica.
Should we greet the morning on yet another note,
Sounding taps to the surrogate snorers
As though we drew a nostrum from their nostrils?—
I see a whole line of images rise:
Such a petal-polish in the barracks!

I love best the evenings of endurance,
The swimmer preened, the sunflower put to bed.
I hear my civilization resting,
The brothers of my being gathered in.
Look in upon us, sir, count the cots:
Chaos is fibrous as the mats we live on.
Now the bugler, silvered in the moonlight,
Has wound our sadness in some safe recoil.

Blind Spot

All of us know the blindfold, how it frees
Us from responsibility and gives
Us the madcap thrill of searching through the dark:
The vase knocked over, the antic pratfall,
The groping in the pillows to a groin,
The silk, and a woman's flesh so savored—
Just being whirled, pointed to the unknown,
Relieves the metaphysical burden.
The bandage removed, one has a blind date
With the world, the broken glass, the flowers strewn,
The stroked girl, dismayed, or coy, inviting,
The terms of proposition, fresh and new.
You have heard another tune while turning,
Dizzy, jumbling the music of the spheres.
You can lay down your own notes on the staff;
They pop like waterlilies from the brain:
Glittering kaleidoscope and arabesque,
The main motif throbbing in the felt thigh,
The song of songs summoned to that bright room—
For once, no ululation down the years,
For a while, your own primordial mix—
It sings and sings, and it will take some time
For the eyes to discover their blind spot
Which may, in fact, seem more like radiance:
The music, the waterlilies, the glamour,
The woman held in the heart's firm blinders,
Even the radio keeps to the score—
We all know these stunned and stunning moments:
The jolt, the jar, the twist of fate,
When you cling so close to the whirling globe,
Open your eyes to let down a planet—
You do not even want the spot to move.

The Mandolin

Why should the nude who is far from thin
Have propped up in her bedroom, against the wall,
The admonishment of the bulbous mandolin?

It stands there like an ancient pear gone to wood.
The long neck that strains for light and music
Says: I, too, have been so long neglected, misunderstood.

The woman's body played upon until she grew stout?—
Did lovers fondle breasts until they hung like fruit
And love's luxurious corpus bottomed out?

Likewise, did the special hand that played the instrument,
Some dark, lean, seignorial man of many parts,
Plucking at her nerves, lose, somehow, his passion and intent?

So the pear shapes of broken hearts—
Perhaps something, out there in the world, gone to seed:
Rooms bare of love, deserted by the arts.

We go on stretching fingers, straining necks,
Hear the music fade, feel the heavy weight descending,
And know what art demands, and love expects.

Red Carpet Treatment

It was a long shot but he would
Walk across a field of poppies dressed in white.
Someone would see the confidence of it,
That he meant to have a red-letter day.
The reality principle was fine
Up to a point: no poppies, no white suit,
All the way up to the edge of the field
Just the frayed hand-me-downs of happenstance,
Then the figure of cream, the Monet glow—
No other suit but the trust in style,

That if you start here you will come out there,
That you can tack down the carpet as you go,
That the unrolled poppies have no backlash:
The girl in a sunhat with a red wave
At her feet, the brilliant diaspora.
I have set this figure on his way before,
The changing room at the very brink of chance,
The summer suit and the long, controlled swoon,
One naked foot testing a spot of blood,
Then the quick, pulled-up power of address,
Like stepping over a ditch just in time.
Even politicians know this impasse,
And roll out the red carpet of rumor.
So lovers regroup at the end of day—
She drops her hat, you a book of verse:
Not until sundown the long, slow roll-up,
The deep sigh in the sun's rubescence—
You have come again to the edge of things.

Tweezers

Pick up the tweezers when you do not want
Too much of anything—an eyelash here,
There, a pebble from the sea, a filling
Of a tooth, the smallest language of things.
How you would like to pick a single word
As if at last you found the *ding an sich*—
After that, tweezers could sleep in the pocket
Like a miner's tool that deserved its rest.

In a secret room, a kaleidoscope
Of magical consort, that glint of gold,
That little boulder from a tooth, the dentist's face
Remembered looking down through the pink cave—
The smoothed glass from the sea, a false sapphire,
The canoe of the lash, the eye water.
One has incredible tremors of desire:
Why not the falling tear, the hung dewdrop?

Sometimes, upright, tweezers have the legs
Of a strait dancer, no gallop, gavotte,
The curving neck, the little mincing head:
The only puppet that our passion knows.
Consider the lover plucking eyebrows,
Somewhere a perfect miniature in view—
Below the mirror, the mounting voodoo,
Imprecations of discarded particles.

Perhaps it is a kind of battle plan,
This animus of fastidious approach:
After the meltdown, just this mosaic—
I can feel it in the fingers, picking
My way, pushing, pushing panorama,
The canoe abreast a pure, perfect day,
The rock replaced in the tourmaline cave—
Ah, says the chary word: Choose me again.

The Clown in the Closet

He does not know just why he loves the moonlight so—
After so much sun, glistening swimmers, the water's startling blue,
Who should glide out of the wings to look at him but Pierrot?

Are there things for which we do not have to ask,
That come out of the woodwork, old closets full of costumes,
That say at some midnight hour: Put on those pantaloons and don
    that mask?

It is not that you will ever let the golden swimmer peel and fade,
But these other moods are never totally put down:
Dark hair, pale face, big buttons, long sleeves, are coming to your
    aid.

Even at the zenith of the day, some fatigue of being you—
One wants wisps of the sea to veil the brilliant girl at your side:
Secretly you milk some gossamer from the overwhelming blue.

Pierrot, mon ami, you whisper in a foreign tongue—
Am I altogether glad to be the person that I am,
Are there figures, moonlit in the psyche, I would rather be among?

But then he dances, departs at dawn—no life fits you like a glove—
Pierrot has been at such great pains to give you this escape,
Much as you found her veils of blue were gone, accommodating
     love.

The Scout in Summer (1999)

I

Eyepatch

It's an obsessive thing, seeing only
Through one eye lying stretched on the sand,
Satin-skinned in between the blue tattoos,
The spread eagle still pinching the shoulder
As if you were not yet free, not yet dropped,
And the claw had a plectrum in it still.
Change hands, the other eye brings meadows back
And a life as modest as violets.
There is a kind of jetty in the brain,
And nothing, for now, gets past the sea wall:
Cornflower eyes, the lover in picture hat,
And you, white-suited don of your desire—
Perhaps a rowing boat, a turquoise lake,
Not yet the thrown, separated savage,
The toothmarks of a snake upon his arm.
One could play at judo with the eyepatch,
There's a long day in anybody's lust:
Now this, now that, one throws one's body weight
As best one can—the oars move on the lake,
The loneliness of the blue-pictured self:
A pitched aesthetic of assaulted vision.
No wonder we speak of ravishing days,
Take pride in how much we carried away.
One should be eyesore when the sun sets red
And the heart beats like a drum at the wall,
An eye for an eye in the twilight.

So lover, now you have me on the mat.
Was it all so that it should come to this?—
A violet magnified upon my chest.

The Albatross

Among all your gains—women, the sea, fruit, art—and not a single
    albatross?—
The list is so compressed it begs another point of view:
There is some expansion, surely one considers loss.

Lips cannot kiss every minute, every hour,
The sea recedes like sexual deflation,
The nose in all its arrogance can never smell every single flower.

Some women promise you no breaking-off, no gap—
Then one glorious afternoon you think is all-out love,
She yawns, a chasm in her mouth, proceeds to take a nap.

Somewhere the long-struck harp is mute—
There are no bridges in the silence of the house,
The pictures pornographic, the table decked with bitten fruit.

There at sea you swear you glimpse a shipwreck—
Your gleaming body says, you say, it still adores the world,
But cannot shake the heavy feeling of a weight around the neck.

Resignation rises in between the close interstices—
Bagged and feeling beaked, you clear the table, gather musty
    clothes,
Kiss the woman wide awake, and make the bird itself pick up the
    pieces.

The Veil of Breath

The man was safely enclosed in an oxygen tent—
Outside, a woman operated a ouija board and rapidly took notes:
It felt as if her hands were on his skin as the planchette moved.

What was she writing about—the past, the present, the future?
How a notorious nomad came to dwell within this tent?
Where were the furs, the rich rugs, the old faithfuls in the harem?

There was no doubt about it, he wanted to be given a reading—
Even his gooseflesh would lend its bumps to those beautiful hands,
The heart-shaped instrument picking up a code from the letters
    and mystical symbols.

Meanwhile, a man with an opthalmascope came into the room
And began looking into his eyes. What had he seen—
The life of a wanderer stored on an intensely colored microfilm?

Under the quick, artificial light, his eyes would sprout again their
    exotic orchids:
He was being coaxed like a palimpsest to grow a new skin—
His night nurse, when she came in, would find his spittle dripped
    ink.

One thing sure about reserved, residual man—
There are those who want to read him near the end
Before paleontology receives the fossil, the print between forever's
    lips.

Some, therefore, presume to gather old men lovingly from park
    benches,
An evening purple glow about them even in the brilliant sun,
Old women still putting eyes in their infinite crochet.

It is better if you can catch them like butterflies before they are
    tented,
Turn them over and over in the mind like a slowed-down
    waterwheel,
As if the river were waiting downstream to be dusted with glitter.

Perhaps it is nothing more than this—a longing for something
    accrued, the life in the envelope—

189

In the old man's vest the amethyst fob with its hypnotic sway,
The needle in and out, more lasting than any hypodermic.

Will our kept and cared-for one roll up the edges of the tent that
    holds the Pneuma?
Those of us on watch indulge the eaves of daydream—pagodas
    and powerful ancestor worship,
Some ancient, ancient menial owning all the secrets of the
    mandarin world.

Splitting Hairs

Maybe it was undivided longing
For the sea, the deep, undiluted hue,
The thing, en bloc, lying still, shimmering,
The pastilles you swallowed, blue placebos
That said you were not getting the message.
Maybe it was her gold hair in a sheath
That was sprayed with implacable lacquer;
Even the complex of your own sun-brown
Body rasping when you rubbed it with oil,
Grown hermetic against the sun's entry—
Purple petunia veins tied at the ends,
The hydrangea fountain stanched in mid-air,
The blue-laden fallback in full stasis.

No wonder you imagine the lapidary
With blue chips on his vest, metal workers
Busy with the artifice of her hair,
As if one strand were Ariadne's thread;
A surgeon who can lift varicose veins
From petunias, pulse them of power,
Release edema from the hydrangeas.

It must be apparent now we follow
With difficulty a single line
Of reasoning and that some pedantry
Is involved, wanting the large and the fine,
Expecting her head whole, handsome, and fragrant

190

And yet a single hair on your shoulder
Alive among the dust and the dandruff:
Home from the labyrinth with this tag end.

Take off the supphose, let the belly's bag
Hang with sapphire, you cannot stir
The sea like blue candy until it ropes
And is ready for desire. You cannot put
A spider on her hair that will draw silk,
Forever let you come and let you go,
Teasing, avoiding the bemused Minotaur.

Sometimes, perhaps, taking your pulse, you think
You have found it, the most finical fuse
That so feeds your delusions of grandeur,
Fades when you lift your hand into the air:
Petunias poised in abrupt transitions,
The heads of hydrangeas dripping in rain—
A gold hair, a brilliant lick of the sea.

The Awl

The man who did not have a belvedere
Conceived one, secret, looking out to sea—
A place to stand naked, wear red briefs
To signal the sea to assignation,
To be somewhat outrageous in private—
And yet finally one waves to the world,
Picks at the far, bright scene as with an awl:
The sharp thrill in the piercing of a day,
The bleeding sea, the brilliant bathing girls—
None of it possible without secrets.
Perhaps all you have is an old shed
Where the fat pigs come to defecate.
Nevertheless, a slow jack is working,
Alive with the lust of colonnaded things.
We sense this lifting process all around
As if a mystery could not manage on its own,
Wanting aqueducts to bring in the sea,

191

The tongue laid on the rim of fountains,
A lizard flicking a tool in his mouth.
Do not tell me you do not sometimes dream
The complex thing—this lunette, alcove, niche,
Fallen circles mimetic round the eyes,
Hung by your neck like a circus acrobat,
Scaling the slick world as a human fly—
By the way, ask the handsome man who looks out
From the belvedere to show you his arm,
The beckoning thing, the red swag concealed,
Smooth as marble to the busy awl.

Granite

Do I feel it in my veins, lungs, kidneys?
Does the mind in me stretch so far and wide?
Can it touch the old, old stone in my heart,
A monument buried in a red cave
Where I have come so often to worship
Like a priest naked in the flowing blood?—
All the while the brain talking to my feet:
The carved altar or the red-light district.

The navel is thirsty for brain-water,
A little whorled, whimsical lake of love.
Straight down into glamour and gut feelings—
Diving, plunging, thoughts filling the sex-pod,
Reaching up, up, into the packed skull—
You pant like a landed fish, until lungs
Are sails swollen with air—orgasmic waters,
The mind not really sure just where it is.

Ferocity of intellect takes charge—
You look at tombstones without sadness:
If not heaven, then not the underworld.
You can command the feet to walk, east, west,
Live sprawling, unlayered—pressure the tongue
To speak a stretched babel of languages.

Nevertheless, sleep comes and you lie out
In a chain of hours, a circle of years—

The omphalos waiting for the sunrise:
The mental heart, the acolyte of stone.
There is a sense that arrows and arrows
Fell by the old rock, cities rose from bone,
And the plains never stopped luring the foot.
All it takes is a rush-sign from above—
Fossilized dendrites quiver, caves open:
The fatal stone is taken by surprise.

The Bend in the River, the Arm of the Cliff

I almost diagnosed myself: emotional wreck—
Thoughts that were not so, feelings that were not true—
Until I saw a swan that wore a black stocking on his neck.

I thought I knew everything there was to know of swans—
If I had been the visual, plastic artist I am not
I could have done them up for you in wood or paint or bronze.

Taking them out of context, the river or the lake,
Pure white, of course, all black, some orange-beaked,
I would give them to you in a chosen medium without mistake.

I could fashion any swan I liked, and mark it: Sold.
The rivers, gardens, yes, the cliffs belonged to me:
I had the edges of imagination well-patrolled.

All in a fantasy, of course, until the day that things went stiff,
Too loose as well, too gone astray, and lacking in decision—
Gardens in turmoil, white water on the river, a figure jumping
        from a cliff.

And then I saw something I had not seen before.
A black-necked swan. It took the turbulence in hand, brought the
        jumper to a halt—
Everything you think you know or fear has another door.

Indigo Oarsman

Like the dragonfly, *Anax junius*,
He felt he was the lord and master of June,
At ease now floating on the river,
Though it had been a long, hard pull upstream,
Full of iron memories, his sweat molten:
A galley slave that long ago escaped
Still drenched with odors of imprisonment,
His blue body like the scull itself.
Could he save ecstasy from the scrap heap,
Tossed out on the banks to rust in the rain?
Go on scraping the blue river for respite
Back and forth, stymied like a chained arrow,
All instruments of freedom longed for, dreamed,
The insect on the water an inspiration?—
The smell of the boat a thick, warm perfume,
His armpits and thighs reeking of resin,
The waterlilies scattered like spittle,
The throat engorged, the halter of muscles,
Cool trees ahead, a cave for convulsion—
The blue slave naming a new country,
The stroked water murmuring an anthem.
Old master, old hand, old heart, slip, slide
Into summerland with the dragonfly.
Take on those dazzling wraparound eyes, see
The far, satin surface you have sewn,
The sutured galley scars, the goaded life—
The river's tongue lapping up nectar,
The broad universe taking a deep breath,
Your muscles leaching what the craft required—
I cannot tell this parable too often:
The blue stretch bilging from the word for home.

II

The Monitor

Evidence abounds, but still only the tip of the world's mistakes,
The cold, deep mass of sorrow and illusion—
I am the man who monitors the moment when the glacier breaks.

Or so I tell myself, these savage summer days.
The ice cube bobbing in the drink is just the southern tinkle
Of some invasive, last, regressive, phase.

I hallucinate the long-pulled thing, up in the air,
French-kiss the icicle, a sword of Damocles,
Making dangerous love to something that is not really there.

The tongue of the panther takes the place of ice—
He has come down to get away from frozen death:
Must I feel the plunge of truth within me, not once but twice?

It is a kind of ecstasy, the far-off knowledge and the nearby pain.
I gulp and nearly choke upon the ice cube:
Another mammoth, northern chunk falls into the sea again.

A glamorous woman in a summer dress assails
Me—My tongue is cold, my skin is hot:
The upper language dazzles, the lower language fails.

The moving world's mistakes, the glittering peak—
I strip, go naked, naked as a roving panther:
The dripping, lolling tongue, the frigid breath upon the cheek.

Tapeworm

This was the young man's only delusion,
Or so he thought, that he had a tapeworm—
Conceived, at first, as knitted in segments
As if he ate part of a white shawl
Hung down where he could altar inwardly.
The heart might even be hierophant,
Letting out the blood to proselytize,
Not knowing the long cloth hid a heathen.

The red wilderness of the intestines
Was not enough, for the disbeliever
Was a pagan who wanted the rich world.
Could the topaz peach be mined by his teeth,
Why couldn't the oaf upstairs swallow the plum whole,
A dark ruby from a sultan's turban?—
That revolting, luscious fire in his mouth
Sends the best food down, lifeless, and overcooked.

One day swimming the young man nearly drowned,
A sudden inward rush of liquid jewel,
The gut at last fully adorned for death.
When they brought him round, he lay stretched out
Handsomely, heavy with lapis lazuli.
Life's beautiful feeders vary their diet—
What should we give to ourselves in secret?
Who let the tapeworm nourish near the heart?

The Loser

If he swims, the thick sea will flatten him,
If he lies on the beach, a cloud looks down.
Even his sex is a heavy nuisance,
Too slung, wanting more girdle and less girth,
His long legs like the stones of a dolmen,
Even his head rolled from someone's tombstone—

This is just a paraphrase of putdown:
Ah, to weep and milk his eyes of marbles.

Now this man is not to be left alone—
He looks too much like a mirror-image
Rolled in from the sea in last night's dream.
Your pitched-in pennies made him powerless.
The ink in your stand looks like his sputum,
His tear is enrosed in the paperweight,
Your body is hung with his rich amours—
How can you rise at right angles to him?

I have thought about these moods at some length,
How the sea nudges, rolls at the bed's edge,
How the blue socks looked sapphired in silt,
The waterglass still as a diamond,
A black pen in the pose of a crowbar.
You could be replaced by a sack of rocks,
You try to sway the cradle of images,
The blue baby harbored in memory.

It may be just a small lifting gesture
As you choose a ring like recovered treasure,
Dangle your father's watch on a safe chain,
Let the shower hose down the hung seaweed,
Look lightly at a picture of past love,
Feel your suit slowly moulting its old stains—
Your arm may still ache from the duffel bag,
But the heart can hum, Rockabye, baby.

You ask all that you can of benefit
From ballast as the long day sways back and forth,
Not minding too much the tug at your sleeve,
The sense of a coffin sliding on ship—
Even the crease, crack, becomes the cradle—
You have good reason rightly to believe,
As you sluice and sluice the swaddled burden,
That the tongue will trill the tip of a wave.

The Necrophile

I cannot imagine why they came to me so juxtaposed,
The rooster and the yellow squash together on the glass-topped
    table,
Unless I felt both live, vulnerable, and totally exposed.

King Cock who never yet had found himself in any serious error
Jumped up toward glimmering gold as if to eat a heap of corn
And found his plucked and yellow body lying there in abject
    terror.

Could this be a comic mirror to his gorgeous red and gold?—
His nude confrere with the curving neck and the head gone God
    knows where
Looked very dead indeed, yet warted with the cold.

Let us go back a step and say I have a very dubious task.
I want to remind the rooster through other means than self
How deep and double every image is, a mask still looking for a
    mask.

The waxen squash laid out as on a glassy catafalque,
Totally rendered as dead rooster, and yet another thing,
Absorbs into its material the red, the rightness, and the will to
    cluck.

I shoo the rooster away for I do not want to see him lost.
He is a foolish, splendid, deciduous thing for a while—so be it:
I eat the squash and keep one image pure at almost any cost.

Epitaphs

What is this death, disorder, that lingers in the head?—
Your house is tidy, and the desk swept clean;
The leaves are raked, the flowers put to bed.

A friend in London died—you sent the wife a cable—
Is there a nagging doubt that you were really friends?

Still, the comity was stretched across the years as far as you were
  able.

You want to keep his epitaph to the point and short,
But every time you try to summarize his life
The fetus of the ego grows and grows, and you abort.

And so the souciance keeps sitting in the mind—
Someone will try to summarize your life some day, somewhere,
And if the child is born at all, no arms, no legs, or deaf, or blind.

Memories abound, abort—more than you can master—
Someone measured in Madrid, another taped in Rome:
Better settle for the photograph smiling at disaster.

Still, that widow in the London flat needs a word or two—
Death, disorder, in our tidy homes—these children of the
  picaresque:
You smile and smile at me, I smile at you.

Gallstone

A bitter word—a harsh reminder—
You have the beginnings of your own stone age:
Kidneys, hardening arteries, the bones,
The slow mineral miasma of the blood.
Sharp pains as you sit quietly reading—
A gastrolith sends you news from below,
The way of the world, lithic after all:
The beautiful blood has gobbets in it.

You wonder about your little treasure.
Could it be marquise, emerald-cut, pear-shaped?
Would a brash lover wear it in a ring?
A dangling fob would be a bit obscene
As if it longed for the secret scrotum
Where it could nestle with a bilious brother.
Would a river of wine wash it away
Or merely delta garnet through the guts?

So you carry in you some extra weight—
The lean topaz man on the diving board,
His sharp surgical jackknife shot with pain,
Never saw the water's belly look so blue,
A simulacrum loaded with sapphire.
How many patients want to let rich veins
When something heavy hovers in their flight?

One has a game plan, one controls one's diet—
Close the jewelry store for good, so you think,
Hope garlic breath rebukes all gewgaws,
As if your gallstone were your deepest bulb,
Packed with death's flowers before it is dug up—
Perhaps meant to be a mini-gargoyle
Lifted into light from sunken days:
Compassion cornered, the grimace of desire.

Stretching the Limousine

After the cocktail party, the drinks and snacks,
When he went outside at sunset to look
At the view, he wanted a spoon of the sea
Like a blue syrup, an inner emollient.
Why can't we have perpetual orgy:
Sex, the forever writing of a poem,
The pulse of the hand on the rich painting?
Why can't we fill up our lives like this?
Inside, he could hear the woman he loved,
But now her voice was a washboard for his nerves—
Just hearing a car on the gravel drive,
Idling, the accelerator pulsing,
Mimicked the imagination at rest.
Another spoon of the sea, then sleep in the nude,
Dream of her hand incomparably soft, deft,
As if it had an unguent in the palm—
Next morning when he drives to work, can he
Trust the first luxurious foot on the pedal?—
The stomach purrs, the heart palpitates,
The sunlight lures us with a virgin day.

It is the mounting thing, we say, that matters—
Back there, the lover, home, the folded clothes—
A spoon on the shelf, the blue tonic waits.
There is a different pressure every day:
Opera is playing in a sidelong car.

The Gilded Cage

The man had been subjected to every kind of shock,
Ill health, a falling market, earthquakes, storms.
And yet, somehow, his brain unfolded like a peacock.

Ah, that glimmering, glistening fan took him by surprise:
Folded, unfolded, stuffed grey and heavy in its case—
How could it look out once more upon the world with brilliant
    eyes?

Hurricanes have eyes, very still, of course—
Health, alas, has many views, back and forth, like Janus;
Markets have a passion for the one-eyed patch: too much delight,
    too much remorse.

The perception of perception goes on and on and on—
I can sit for hours, eyes closed, dreaming in the sun,
Wondering if there will ever be again a peacock on the lawn.

Yes, mayhem, thoughts of murder in the selfsame brain—
The light, that subtle artist, keeps working in the deepest sources
    of our sight—
Relax, relax. Stop holding back the implications of an iridescent
    stain.

Health may be impaired, storms regroup, markets change their
    patches:
Pavanes abound, and stately homes go down,
But a bird is roosting in your mind that nothing in the world quite
    matches.

III

Once Around the Ego with the Id

Imagine, if you will, a bamboo grove,
The green leaves, and the silver on the ground.
Introduce some peacocks and a small pond
Turbulent only with waterlilies.
Invite for a later time that evening
Harlequin, his mandolin, love's music.
All you need to do now is to provide
The profound "I" which is strangely missing.

One does not have to be a passion-monger
To see that nothing will happen unless
The profound personage arrives, imbued:
Aware of the great fan of the bamboo
That waves, cools off the face of God himself,
Trained to show a blue tongue to the peacocks,
Ready to light the lilies like burners,
Lush with the antics of Harlequin in hand.

So be it, then. You deploy some evidence.
You have met up with some few matching parts,
You have dared to announce your proposal—
It need not be nearly as composed as this,
Just an unmistakable grasp of language,
Viewing a lover's bloody handkerchief—
A red poppy, and a torn scarlet scarf:
That, too, could be a cue for an entrance.

I have looked for myself quite long enough,
And the great surge is the thing to wait for.
It knows when and if Harlequin can come,
And lifts up the fan to a long-tired god.
You do not need civil tongues, only blue,
When you come to loot my house and leave.
I am burning incense on a lily:
It matters only that you catch my drift.

Restaurant by the Sea

The man was exhausted but suddenly relaxed: he felt happy, he
    felt well—
It would not throw him if he should open clean white oysters at a
    table
And find dead ears, in their liquid of sorrow, lying on the shell.

This is the man, you see, who has swallowed a pound of grains
And no matter what you set before him he will delve and find a
    pearl—
Why split the mind so often if you cannot count upon a little
    something for your pains?

Make him do it then, make him show you how as long as he is
    able—
Bring him a bucket of blue-lipped, recalcitrant clams,
Leave a knife, a napkin, and little else at your dour table.

He will bend down and lend an ear to all those saturated ears,
Tap with his knife: May I come in, your friendly, local surgeon
Who has learned at the end of a long, hard day not to be queasy
    with your fears?

How to be limpid, life-loving, and totally without qualms!—
So many people sit us down at bleak, uncompromising *table d'hôte*
To find the pearl when none is there, for those extended palms.

I have known hard days and sat alone, curiously alive, in a sad café,
Been given a knife to rap on the table like a medium for
    messages—

A pearl, a plate of ears, at the end of my strength and what have I
    to say?

The Dream Book

A man with a packet of pencils
Is drawing a picture of cleansed veins,
Those flush, ravishing inroads of the sea.
To lay down the day like a fresh blue coast,
The pencil moves as supple as seaweed—
How soon it wanders off the page, picks up
The filaments of discarded days
As if a blue wire coruscated colors,
As though we pulled a hot line to instinct:
The glorious nude umbilical with gold,
Flowers ringing with received messages,
The picture plugged in with glow and power—
A dose of the sea and you become this draftsman.
I doubt if your pharmacologist will give
You more than one blue pill a day. He knows
How the bowels bleed from too much boisterousness,
How we sit at the desk, seethe with the sea.
Still, I do believe in self-prescription
When heart needs washing in a violet wave.
I have a whole stack of them, blue-bound books,
These old, old directories of desire,
The latest one still open and loose-leaf,
The rapt tongue with a recent trace of blue
As if sputum broke on infinite shores.

Arms and the Man

What are we to do with everything amiss?—
Turn off the television, turn down the radio, trash the papers,
And sit on the porch this summer night and smell the clematis?

anked, bent over like a static fountain in the moonlight,
t pours its scent and goes down deeper in the senses
'han any momentary wish I have to set things right.

see a woman in the moonlight, I see a marble stair:
'he clematis is urging me to fantasize
.nd ask: How can the heart be given everywhere?

'he pistol and the bomb are always ready with their fire—
Vill she throw white roses down the steps to me?
Iow can I grovel to my heart's content at the bottom of desire?

am picking up the roses, planning my ascent—
f I turn on the news, will the white fountain straighten like a
    rocket,
:ombining echoes of the dream-abandoned town with my intent?

'he flower, the stair, the moonlit launching pad—
.m I blending back together in the deepest depths of scent
'he force of the world and some great passion to be free of it I
    had?

The Sponge

t had ambitions to suck in the sea,
Not just a wave but the whole vast ocean:
'he inward rush of that blue ecstasy,
Remembering perhaps where it once lived,
'he subversive in it now grown monstrous,
. personality change born on land—
:omplex history has gone from wet to dry,
'he reduced circumstances of bathroom life.

.till animus weds its own anima—
'he lovely woman in her blue bathtub,
:areless, comfortable, in a pearl choker,
Vanting all things that have come from the sea:
iqueezing the wet sponge in an act of love
Jntil it pours soft pearls all over her,

And the wretch must gasp and drink its own suds,
Lonely alcoholism of the ocean.

Later, perhaps, a little sly vengeance,
Slithering onto the merciless tile
Where she steps down and is jarred by a wave,
Venus, too, remembering her origins—
But she picks up the little souse and shakes
It for any last, hidden bubbles:
The sink is the place for sex offenders,
And he must lie there in his own spent sperm.

Still gender is lost when the sun comes through
The window and the loins of the lover
Go dry again, the arid mind regrets
Its insatiable lust for images.
But the sponge is an old recidivist,
And cannot resist the smallest water—
Put it again in your lover's warm hand,
And feel the pearls gathering in the brain.

The Center of Attraction

When he looked through the brilliant window of the indoor pool,
He could see the ghost of a turkey cock waddling, weaving toward
   him
Where he stood naked to receive this glorious November illusion.

It was like a galleon coming to float in his own private water,
As though his body unabashedly beguiled a fierce and luxurious
   impression,
Something, stored with autumn, that he would wrest from the
   world by main force.

If the heart and mind have no power like a magnet,
Every season will go by and you will never have captured cargo:
It is listless to look through a window and make no golden leaf a
   barge.

206

Perhaps for you it is the deer striking the barred light of the sun,
Making such music, as if the sky were hung with cymbals,
Your heart waiting like a tympanum where the leaping hoofs will
    land.

Yet another wakes beside the woman he loved, throats filled with
        the glut of golden flower
As if Aaron had been shaking his rod above them all night long,
Having asked to be gorged and gorged forever on miracles.

This much is certain—you must be in some way attractive:
Let the beetle linger on your finger in amber and make a scarab,
Pull down the honey into the mouth like a long, loquacious tongue
    of pleasure.

You will not, believe me, ever suffer image-burn—
The ship shaped like a bird comes in, deposits its splendor,
The pool quivers with coins, the thought of gold is thoroughly
    shaken down.

You have lured the world, but did not really loot it—
There is not a mark on the naked swimmer as he moves in liquid
    bullion.
Still, as he dries himself, how stored he looks—the towel drops as
    if heavy with his likeness.

Now, as the sun goes down, inking the room one last time with gilt,
What is this powerful urge to be fingerprinted except to tell
That what you took disburdened or disparaged nothing,
    belonged, in trust, to no one but yourself.

IV

Conversation at Dawn

You know his story as you know a moving picture—
He was a handsome man, an athlete, an artist:
He had held himself together perfectly for several decades.

He could sit in his garden where the phlox glowed like scepters
And the pool was a sapphire lode he mined with his body,
A rather golden-looking man, a well-honed tool, in his crisp, white
  suit.

The house looked placed there powerfully by no other hand than
  his.
There was a portrait on the wall like a change of clothes:
The artist had seen him as a man who walked into his suit

Totally intact—He could line any flimsy thing with instant marble.
It was remarkable, the monumentality combined with kinetic
  thrust:
Every man in the room with sloppy socks longed for garters,
  abdominal belts.

Even a ray of sun seemed to present itself like a safe—
The hand turning in the light looked absolutely fabulous:
He was the only man who could successfully rob himself.

Though birthdays brought him nothing but cards To The Man
  Who Has Everything,

In an increasing effort of will, he tried to remember who he was:
Some days, when no one was looking, he talked to his portrait.

Elegant, graceful, jocular—That's what the painting said—
And so the implacable echo began to get to him:
Perhaps it was time to let the original enemy return.

He came unwillingly, of course, a boy in dirty underwear.
They talked until dawn, exchanging tips on living, possible
    vacations,
Polite, apologetic about status, the persona, the person that hurts.

Bull's-Eye

It was too warm to be a rapt voyeur,
The view too open: pond, meadow, glimpsed sea.
Yet I longed for the hole, the slatted sight,
A tumid eyeglass that could square a frame.
The girl did not know this, and would not care
Perhaps to be kidnapped, singled out, withdrawn.
She took a walk on a hot summer day,
Having her own occasion, sense of style—
A modern girl but in a long white dress,
Pink scarf, a parasol from an old trunk,
All like an encyclical of the past.
But what it lacked was me, yes, monstrous me,
Implacable, heavy with heat, shadow,
The need for sudden report unbearable,
The sound of a man shot from a canon
Landing on his feet in another's mind.
The girl turned, looked my way as if she heard,
Saw nothing but the thick trees, sauntered on.
I stood still, tense, cocked, encapsulated,
I could not forgive the world its silence—
There would be no show now or any day.
The pond, meadow, the meretricious sea
Told me, yes, monstrous me: Make do, make do.
At just that moment the girl paused and smiled,
Her parasol like a white parachute

Which she might lend me for my swift descent.
Nothing more—but the great gun kicked, went off—
I had this illumined picture in my arms,
Powerful, soaring, aimed. The girl looked up:
I could swear she made her heart the target.

Tiger, Tiger

Late afternoon, the hunt—still the tiger means to spring.
My stripes invisible, the marks of tooth and claw,
I roam the room as if I meant to keep on prowling.

One languishes, rolls, temporizes in the sun—
I sit at the desk, naked in the light, haunches, hands, electric:
The hunt for words, phrase, feeling, thought, is never done.

Men in their seventies must stay animal:
Lips, breasts, fruit, wine, orgy, orgasm—
They are not, you tell yourself, gone for good, beyond recall.

The mind says yes, yes, yes, but there's a rub:
The lady leaves, the fruit has spots, the head hungover—
You cannot treat the world as if it were forage for a cub.

I rise, put on a dressing gown striped like a tiger's skin,
Or is it just the sunlight coming through the blinds?
Blind ambition? Transfers of the golden youth worn a little thin?

Sit down, put a line of words across the page, a bar—
Another and another. This is the cage old men look through,
And you will see them as you wish and as they think they are.

Pierrot

His head in the frilly white collar
Looks served on a platter of confectioner's whipped cream,
Something left over from the reign of terror.
Then as he moves he is everyone's pale,
Life-sized, floppy doll. Ah, Pierrot,
We say, you have escaped, you have survived.
Mother put you to bed within your body,
Father, smoking his cigar, wreathed in dreams,
Tiptoed by the door and, casting off his clothes,
Wondered why his flesh had grown so thick.
Supple in the moonlight, garments thrown across a chair
Wait to dance with Pierrot. There is no one
Who does not remember these interstices
Where even the languid cat rolled himself
Into a muff to accommodate a stifled laugh
And the clock in the hall monumentalized
The roguish life that underneath the surface lurked.
It may be hard to make up anything discrete
From the filmy gauze of such imponderables,
But, sitting at breakfast, Father with the news,
Mother with her cup of whitest porcelain,
The children's eyes like sleepy pools of darkness,
All know that they will play their other game
All through the brilliant day hung with tatters—
Wanting a smile that looks like Pierrot's,
Watching a walk that's made of silk and sticks,
Finding a head that floats above its life,
Laughing, amorous, fed like a water lily,
As if it knew why some things live forever.

Notes of a Native

If your mind wants to go a certain way,
Why not let it for a change?—the pink phlox,
The bird bath, sunset, the dream of Eden,
A ravishing woman dressed in pink silk,

The dream clothed now, and pulled as far as here.
In the bedroom a halo of photographs
Round the mirror recalls the journey
Like the headdress of a peering savage—
You have looked for this place all of your life.
Sometimes the bath encapsulates the sea,
And she shimmers with green, aquamarine,
The late sky depilated of all clouds.
Just to one side, you stand on the doormat,
Thinking of closets filled with throwaways:
Will the fringed mirror swallow one more time,
Leaving on its rim pictorial smears?
The evening replies and turns harlequin,
Enplums the sky, empurples the woman,
The phlox look heavy as goblets of wine.
Before the stars pin the day into itself,
Staking the whole thing for the late savage
Like a scraped skin of time stretched out to dry,
Let me insist once more on this method,
Much as you have pinned notes on the kitchen wall
To remember to remember when you rise,
The indigene of your own insistence.
I have fondled and fondled the woman,
But that is another story—a clue
In language itself will lead you beyond
The garden to the quake in the bedroom
Where the mirror swallows, swallows, the world.

The Unabashed

A bowl of apples in the sunlight and I the nude—
They made a contradictory combination:
The hard, sunburned, almost metallic man, the fleshly food.

If you come upon us suddenly, you might wish to claim
Us for a painting, still life, but not too still—
Call it the moment of the apple and the man, and put it in a frame.

Just so, the world is activated by surprise—
You happen on the man, totally nude, the voluptuous fruit,
And are called upon to make them slave and captive of your eyes.

With the man, of course, you take a risk—
He could stand up, glare, walk right out of range—
Red-breasted apples then would lose their charm: no man around,
    no odalisque.

I wonder if we do not prowl the world to find
Pictures that we think belong to us—
That mountain through the window: you walk and walk to prove
    you are not blind.

Therefore, never fear when you are come upon—
It is gracious to be naked, and glorious to want apples:
The moment frames you for a moment, and you belong to
    everyone.

V

The Scout in Summer

For some time now the man has felt hung, stuffed
In a golden bag. His body is lean and hard
But he feels like a spider, all belly,
Still luxurious in a way, therefore gold,
But envenomed, a fat drop of malice.
No one on earth would ever see him so.
He looks like a sinew of the universe—
We would say he gathered the net of life
Into his body, a packed parachute.
His fall from a cliff would be slow, solid,
Making the stones resilient as rubber.
We count upon him as our only god
To release us, people closed in closets.
But for some time now the scout has held the knob,
Paunching his image, letting out the net,
Fingering the loose possibilities,
Considering the brute reverse of things,
Wanting to leave his skin-suit on a chair
Limp as a Dali image, go off hard,
Alone somewhere, and then to inspect himself
Where nature does not need his minute love—
It was the simplification that he loathed
At the same time that he pared its clearest form,
A curious, opaque, yet see-through, man,
Holding out the spotless fruit of summer,
An unwilling god of closet-people—

So handsome in hubris, tossing the string
To the first one who wants to store the net
Or will meet him where it lies in a heap
Like the bunched entrails of illusive form.

Jump Start

When you think you have finished with desire,
Lava erupts like the yolk of an egg
Aborting a million firebirds—Some sparks,
However, fly back to jump start the heart.
When you think the sea has chilled your groin,
There you are like a gas burner in blue.
When all the sunflowers are burned-out faces,
You shake and shake them for their pollened tears.

Think of yourself therefore as tangible
And vital among your own creations,
Someone very good at job analysis,
Someone who has let the huge juggernaut
Of facts go back and forth over him
And caught sparks from the caterpillar treads.
You see, the message of the egg was cast
Far and wide, fireflies pulse with afterglow.

Reconsider that figure of the gas burner—
Have you not felt luxuriously warm in the sea
Like a heated, golden coil of desire,
Standing on sand, calling hands to stroke you,
All ready to light the wick of the world?
Nor will you ever forget those weeping
Faces—Can they go on storing up their grief
Whenever your warm hand lets down their heads?

Ashes, the snuffed pilot light, dried brown eyes,
Of course, but in the back of the old car,
Always, the jump cable. You may see me
Rattling round some days—Then the egg explodes,
The pilot lights and the cold sea sizzles,

The flowers release their cisterns of tears—
You look beautiful there among lit images:
Come touch me—I am warm and thrilling too.

Manatee

To have been told as a child there were mermaids and now
To see the sad, blubbery mass moving on the screen,
To be judged on how I handle an appointment with a sea cow!

The men from the boys they say—This is where one conquers or
   one fails:
Embrace fatty degeneration as one loves a bloated wife,
Revert to childhood, reinforce with sequins a picture always losing
   scales.

It takes some doing, this retrograde but fabulous collage:
The fat wife is encouraged to corset and to paint,
This always and forever standing by, holding up an image.

Better to let her roam those murky meadows of the sea—
Who is to say how much, how little, where the balance
Whereby we can negotiate between the mermaid and the
   manatee?

Perhaps the whole thing comes down the mountain of desire, the
   bobsled and the luge,
When the strained corset bursts in metastases of flesh,
And all the smiles and all the wiles founder under too much rouge.

Still, I love the sea, the figure on the rock—I blow a kiss—
Though more is tumbled down, the mountain streaked with blood,
We still must arbitrate how much the thing itself, how much the
   artifice.

The Flash Point

Was it the last chartreuse, one glass too much,
That produced the vague green mist in the mind?—
Even cannibals want to float their dinners,
The undigested flesh rising on blood
As if the tropic stomach had icebergs.
One wants this having eaten well to fade
A bit, become loose, luminous with thought:
That red glow, this Marvellian green light.

There is a certain saintliness in this,
The primitive urge to regurgitate,
The refined ether forming in the brain.
One can read that red retching in the sun,
Or treat the head as if it were pilot
For a gas ring—You may light it or leave it.
There is nothing to equal the mind's fumes,
Dangerously inhaled, or cooking the meat.

Be careful, *cabotin,* but not too careful—
The caveman shaves his way into manhood,
The glutton has his notion of glory,
From head to foot we are ripe, rife, with risk—
I have lit these full men after dinner,
Gone home with burn-marks of their nimbus,
Or felt the sick, wallowing savage look
To the sunset to flare and light the stars.

The Niche

It was an accumulated thing—first
The sides coming in closer, the blue dome
Coming down, substituted for the sky,
Until it was like an open, upright
Sarcophagus—daybed for the daimon.
In his much lighter moods he could suppose
It was the blue nacelle of a balloon

Which had grazed the earth but was not grounded,
Still tumescent, the tugging, sky-blown shroud.
No wonder he sat under the dryer
As often as he could, his hair streaming
As though his heavy seat were an outrigger
That could move, move forward, and never tip,
Picking up lithe, caressive images,
The touch of passing fingers, lint of love,
Before the blue wash turned hyacinthine
And sat on his head like a hard, jeweled cap—
So you have signed your name to a recess
And are posed among electrostatic
Incidents, feeding, crowding the inset.
A breast passes by and is firmly grasped:
So much buoyance, so much powerful surge;
The luscious lips stick and roll back the tomb.
We want immense ballast—at the same time
Keep blasting, boosting the stone for lift-off.
The watch under the plastic dome dangles
The predicament—We are bagged with time.
I heard a lark in the niche one day.
It had flown up from the nest of my head,
A song, a beating that freed the bubble—
One hand held to his foot, the other
Dragging my ball and chain. I did not want
Quite yet to sign my name to anything,
Stretched and fueled by neologisms,
The body and its basket filled with hands.

Ladybug

Some day when you are down and feeling dour,
Give up majestic scenes, magnificence, the magna-thing:
Your conflicts can be solved in miniature.

Arms could not quite reach around the world and hug—
A sea spilled over, a continent herniated:
It was time to take your troubles to the ladybug.

The spots upon the back, the glowing orange color—
A *tachiste* of singular skill and grace
Never wandered from her tiny work in search of an expansive
    dolor.

You can count on it. *Weltschmerz* will come again:
The spur, the arched incredible, the Lippizaner—
Meanwhile you pet the hip-high little creature with the flowing
    mane.

Thus, we slide the rule, trifle with the golden mean—
The ladybug goes right on looking beautiful, munching pests,
Working overtime: little syntheses keep our great ambitions clean.

In time, we mean to hug the world, of course—
Handsome rider, dressed up for your highest thoughts,
All the while, down below, we trained and trained the little horse.

Strings

Should one be subtle even at the end
Or use the rough ropes of experience?—
The world you knew an angled crazy quilt,
The small seams sewed here and there by bird feet,
The magic and the merde smeared everywhere.
You want to haul it in now, have it all
In the bag, a tramp who thinks he is a toff,
The fat twist dangling from a bending stick.

Still the nerves keep twitching at odd ends:
A sunflower, dazed, falling from the cloth,
Crushed, rubbing the shag of earth with gold.
You are still sutured somewhere to the sea,
A purse-seine lying just beyond the wound,
No hawser thick enough for happiness.
It is the overlapping thing one loves
As the sea boils and boils its buoyant blue.

So say it out flat—the unpulled woman
Floats on the longest stretched-out line of all,

The amniotic sac of ecstasy—
You can miss the touch of her actual hand
As she lies still unborn in your warm bed.
There are times though when the gathered feeling
Makes the body a glorious catchment,
Sun, sea, tucked in by the silk feet of birds.

VI

Coral Reef

As if it were a sea that roves and sieves, belief
Is infinite, filled with little creatures of the mind
That, almost unknown, almost against their will, build up a reef.

After some time, you may seem even to yourself somewhat cut-
    and-dried,
But the mass, submerged, actually desirous and unstable,
Keeps growing on thoughts that gave their best and died.

Therefore, the sea, forever free, but here and there contained,
Lets these underwater castles go on building—
Why should anything so vast have hindered or complained?

No wonder swimmers rise, refreshed, compact and pink—
They have swum all over the castles' tourmaline
And never had to give a harsh or hardened thought to what they
    think.

The girl who lingers over what to wear—necklace? ring?
Or both?—may not know that she is always fishing in her past—
Perched forever on themselves, the sequined mermaids sing.

Still, castles have their crags, swimmers cut themselves, women sag
    beneath parure—
Why do we wash the bleeding finger, drop the jewels in the box,
Except to say we know our days are pliant but the reefs endure?

Hydrangea

So heavily blossomed, if one should cut
A bloom, two others crowd in, replace it.
I think of Hydra, many-headed snake,
Even the blue eyes muffled in sequins,
Shimmying in the wind. The mind skips again:
A huge glittering ball in the disco,
A serpentine girl waving her slim hips.
What are we looking for? When? Where? Why?

The dancing boy weaves like a snake charmer,
A reptilian odor under his armpits,
Having been bitten over and over by love,
Immune, so he thinks, to her mouth's liquid
That turns in an instant to pure venom.
I barely touched the bulging hydrangea
In passing, and all of this, all of this:
A packed head and a scrotum full of sequins.

Both thought, desire, are taut but stretch themselves—
A sense of old snakeskins blown everywhere:
Adonis of the disco, the damp Venus
Up from the waves, smelling of sea-serpent—
At midnight, the confetti, the squama,
Climax, orgasm of the groined ceiling—
So, I am an escort of ecstasy,
Hydrangeas fondled like paramours.

Are the old myths still floating in the air,
Looking for a mind, groping memory
For fossils? Hollow exoskeletons,
Invisible miasma of spent skins—
I touch the living girl in a blue dress,
My dazzled head turns like a glittering ball:
Adonis, the grip of the ancient snake,
Tongue of a thirsty concept slaked with seed.

Sack Race

When the great queen shook her beautiful head,
One expected a dandruff of diamonds,
So the sophist said, but he was wrong—
She knew how to carry the glittering weight,
She bowed without tipping the tiara
As if roots and stems grew up from her brain.
Somewhere the seismograph wrote its crabbed hand,
But it was a dead letter to the queen:
Not a brilliant spattered, a pendant dropped.
Out on playing fields they run the sack race,
Taking down into their legs the lust for poise,
Those with their spit curls and pierced earlobes,
Jumping as if sacks were weighted with jewels,
Daring the men to bare their knives and scythes—
In the crowd, the safecracker's keen, lewd eye.
Perhaps it began long ago, this desire
To go to the far end without falling,
Started in feet and thighs—tied at the waist,
The human lump made sinuous, supple,
A crooked sigma pausing in the grass
While the quick breath comes in like smelling salts.
The queen when she was young must have seen it,
Must have frisked the palace columns for support,
Felt a rush when the robust girl came through—
The prisoners in their shackles heard and cheered—
I can never see a snake fence in the field
Without saying, here we go, there we go,
One more stride and the legs will be gowned,
The hair swept up, the head crowned with sunlight—
The boys at hurdles, the hanging scrotum—
The old queen, at last, buried in diamonds,
Will plant this pleasure in a sacred place.

The Fingernail

It lay there lifeless like a brittle boat,
A little cutting from his finger—
More work with scissors, then a flotilla
In drydock but wanting the open sea.
Imagination will do anything to sail:
A hair fallen becomes a golden rope—
Could we let ourselves down into some cave?
Does the bland surface yield to every thought?

That white fleet, that rope, the cave and the sea,
The wit and the power of Prussian blue
As if Hokusai loved your outspread hand,
And gave you coast and sea to sail upon.
Comb your hair and excavation begins,
You will dangle from something of yourself.
Archeology and seafaring are there:
You cannot be held back, restrained, called home.

So it seems to you for a packed moment,
Artists and artisans wandering in your mind.
The brush, the wind, blunder onto the scene:
The wreck of the ships, the slip of the rope.
The fingernail grows again, the hair thickens—
I feel a bow in the palm, a handshake,
The lust of the cave lies deep in the scalp:
Over and over, delved and outward bound.

Missing Link

Perhaps it was a smell of violets on her fingers,
A touch of blue about her face, a magic haze—
Perhaps a blue moon passed me long ago, but lingers.

How many things have only paused, then taken flight?—
It seems ages, another world, another dispensation,
I saw and heard her playing Chopin in the moonlight.

It was then I kissed her fingers, brushed her face,
Lit the lamp, found her standing all in blue,
Saw deeper, past her through the window, how the moon can race.

Something told me even then that all was lost,
That it would come to nothing, a vignette of the moment,
And I would waken in the morning to bruised beginnings and blue
     frost.

For it never ceases, does it, never can quite end?—
This seeing something almost perfect: the girl, music, moonlight,
That expectations of amours always meant to blend.

Many rooms, many sounds of music, violets—
Life is a string of unforgettables, alas detached:
How to make them last? One thinks one knows a moment and
     forgets.

Reading the Leaves

Have you sometimes wondered if autumn's fortune
Could be better told with tea leaves, reduced
In a cup, the sadness, the fire's soaring,
The ash that dreams an albino landscape?—
It is the rich imbuement that cannot last:
The leaf on the hand like a splayed birthmark,
The veins pulsing their fat caterpillars,
The jugular coursing with memories of wine,
The having tasted, taken in so much,
The threat of not quite metamorphic glut—
When will the death-wish settle in the cup?—
Come flexure, come twister, come rising wind.
See, the golden mounds shift like trembling graves,
The sudden dervish of a released spirit.
The gutters whisper from their cluttered lips,
Predict that the swamped car escapes in time,
While the leaf-sweeper swills its motley drink.
A worn and rusted man stares at the dregs,
Wants to be malleable, to be bent,

Folded over, hinged, cut into slivers,
In love with piecemeal prophecies—
I would need the thin membrane of the ox
Goldbeaters use for layering their leaves
To have enough to gild these many moods:
The sunset that lacquers its bloom on my skin,
The fruit that rolls over on its rotten spot,
The wine juice going brown in the scuppernong—
So I turn in the world's distribution—
Do not ask me the wish of tomorrow:
I sway and swerve in the flair of the leaves.

Calipers

When you have been measuring the thickness,
The thinness of things for so long, you will
Feel like Harlequin, cut off at the trunk,
With his legs spread, standing in the moonlight,
Head, body, somewhere drifting in the air,
Leaving the dark earth to its own lump sum—
Why did you have such metal in the soul
So that you must take the measure of things?

It would have been enough merely to dance,
Pull the skein a bit, touch the shimmering skin,
Drenched by the wave with a blue orgasm,
No worry about rapture of the deep—
Slide the hand along the lover's warm hip,
Cantilevered over the Great Desire:
If you fall, come up like the cat burglar
As far as the closed windows of her eyes.

It is perfectly true the surface slips
And slides, and the raw, skinned world quivers,
Flaps and flaps of blue, and the eyes plundered.
That is why your legs wait in the moonlight:
They want the head to come home, the heart to settle.
Then you will be deep in the damp and dew

226

By morning, earth-steam rising to the crotch—
How thick the aura of our ancient love!

The Dagger of Degas

Why not put down your pen as the painter finally does his
     brush?—
The pen dipped in places some people would not put their
     umbrella.
Life was so mixed, manic, clean, dirty, beautiful, and lush:

The gossip, the scandal-mongering, the listening at the door—
Though she stands handsome, upright, in exquisite gown,
That day the painter had her stretched out naked on the floor.

You wrote of wine, women, sun, sea, peaches,
And lifted them above the fast-moving, noisome stream
Which sucked and sucked as if it hung you with a bag of leeches.

So, after all, a swan went flooding on your dolor
As though it held your heart upon its wings—
Across town, the painter stabbed, revived, stabbed, revived the
     model, his brush loaded with color.

There must have been times though without reach: no swans,
     ecstatic train—
The sewer seems to rise and rise and rise,
And the *quid pro quo* of life and art will never work again.

Some day, some far day, one hopes, they part—
The swan, if there was a swan, serene, with just a glance of menace,
Will never tell exactly what it was to bear the burden of a heart.

The Gyroscope

What happens to the too constricted mind,
Throbbing with golden swimmers, sea, sand, palm?—
Onshore, women bottled in stale perfume,
The last kiss, a butterfly fluttering off.
Violets suck for color in the veins,
The fountain, choked, mortified, and silent:
The random images we all rehearse,
The skull too small for such a story line.

The morning glory calls for admission,
A flowered snake twining around the throat.
The hurt sea slaps you as you pass by.
The last, shameful kiss lights on a dungheap.
Swimmers doubled in pain lie at your feet
As if poisoned by their own golden glow—
So you accept the flower's admonishment,
Make room for the wrapped morning suppliant.

A truce at last, a rare, rushed transcendence,
The prestidigitation of closed space—
I look in wonder at a walking man,
A smile, a tear perhaps, but little else
To show his store of exits, entrances.
Pause, pause, and beautify the butterfly,
Let the violet milk and milk your chest:
The sway of the world itself supports your swoon.

Snow Leopard

You cannot, though you love it, live only in the sun:
Coral islands, palms, voluptuous girls, blue sea—
How can mind, at last, deal with our abandon?

It is not enough, the pink-blushed island slant with rain,
The flamingos, gray, their necks like plumber's tubes:
The leopard seems the right resource if we would live again.

Before the islands, I saw him some time very long ago,
Calling to my rich, anemic, heart to seek him out,
Powerful, imperturbable, standing green-eyed in the snow.

Is the leopard, then, my twin in the dream of being whole?
Does he come in at night, eat the fruit, paw the girls, pull the blue
    rug out from under me?
Antipodal, just before sleep, I see him running, leaping from the
    other pole.

I tossed, turned, reached out to clutch the flamingo's neck,
    draining pink,
Saw the lime-green marbles of those eyes glowing in the dark,
Filled through the gut and spilling into day a cleanser in the sink.

I cannot walk away from them, his rough tongue and those green
    eyes—
I hear the burbling drain, see the bird, startling pink as sudden
    dawn:
The snow-capped mountains moved last night and brought the
    white antagonist to my blue paradise.

The Existentialist

Just turn the rowel on your lavish mind
Until it quivers—a poinciana
Awakened to a clear and brilliant day.
Let a dazzling birdsong be your trumpet,
The ear miming with its own whorled form,
That slender beak pushed down deep in nectar,
The little howitzer of happiness
That fires its iridescence in the nerves—
This, we hope, a first and not the last trump—
We do not seek Procrustean pleasures:
Just poinciana like the brain's fountain,
The bird feeding and firing in the ear,
No short limbs stretched too far, none cut off,
No heinous hacksaw hidden in the heart—
Thus, the man that morning obsessed himself,

229

Found a thread of blood along the razor
Like a red filament of a flower,
Drew a pencil across the plot of earth
Where his shadow was buried yesterday.
Do not tell me you have not tried to be
Some day the man you really want to be:
A flowering tree in your head, bird-infused,
A bright flush on your chest like a breastplate,
The pubis ablaze in tight underwear—
Friend, it will do you no harm to follow
An image to the bottom of itself.
You must live somewhere on just such bedrock,
Clutching your own pyxidium of pictures.
Thus you can call Proserpine at will.
The wind blows strong some days, some days falls short.
You alone can know the weight of the seed.

The Jogger by the Sea (2002)

I

The Body on the Sand

Destiny is out there somewhere, the blue sea,
The black rocks, the sprawled, bruised, wave-tossed figure.
One has not seen him, but knows that he is there:
Condoms, a place where people have had sex,
Around the corner, a cove of desire,
Bikinis left behind, a pair of shorts.
Suicide comes to mind, except that he is nude:
Did he dive from the ship as deep as hoped?

The hidden cove is a leveling place:
Tryst upon tryst, trash on trash—a balance,
Black rocks defend and guard, defend and guard,
And yet the sea brims, and brims voluptuously:
The suction of my pen swells in my pocket.
Must I, alone, be the one to find him,
Simulacrum of a higher passion,
Am I the litterbug of lost loves?

Above, a helicopter grazing for the dead—
It is time to be oh so laconic,
Waiting for the umbilical cord to come down,
Having come too far and not far enough:
Too many pictures savored just like this,
Backed with postures and sublimations.
The black, black gate and the blue forever.

I speak of stark and quivering moments,
Oscillations, edges, diasporas—
Some other summer day I saunter there,
Holding a girl by the hand, pressing the sea—
Nothing, no one there—then the long, deep kiss,
A filament, a fetching-up of us
Somewhere, our bodies pulled and foundered:
This time, overhead, blades like angel's wings.

Riding the Sunset

Every day it looks as though the sun has died
Toward evening, slowly diving, glaring red,
Too full of the hot afternoon, the passions overfed:
Mallarmé said that it committed suicide.

A lingering death, then, the long rubescent dive—
No headlong, desperate, manic swimmer,
It enters the sea still glowing, dwindles to a glimmer,
Cooling off the earth, whatever is alive.

Some of us who live by fortune, chance,
Could wish the sunset had more dash—
Self-sacrifice with spectacle and splash,
If it had the startling mission of a lance.

Therefore, watching, we must carefully choose our words,
Those that reflect, reflect upon each other's facets:
The brilliant, solitary, phoenix in us never quite forgets—
Last night was just as calm with settling birds.

The chance, always, no dawn, no iridescent start—
A risk that Mallarmé was right,
Right because his deadly prophecies delight:
Words that slowly ride the sunset down into the heart.

Hammock Hyperbole

Lying in a hammock, watching the girl
Twirling in the blue leotards, the sea
In the distance whipping up a blue mousse,
You are so relaxed that it all seems
To come from you. She is like a butterfly
That you have released—any minute now,
Your lips for nectar, and stretched there, and topped
With cream, the rich, delectable dessert.
Even a caterpillar does a slow
Cakewalk toward you, measuring your mood:
Not too many opinions in the bag,
Not too many angular attitudes,
Even the motor of memory at rest—
You want to spread out the mesh of your nerves,
Let the whole loose net loll in loveliness,
The body itself stretched between rich trees,
The sackload both luxurious and light—
But, in fact, the dancing girl will not let
You lie there forever, or the whipped waves
Keep tempting appetite. It is the sport
Of course who will be forever turned out,
Over onto the ground, bruised with images.
Still, there are blackberries close by, the juice
Of the injured sea, black grapes for frosting,
And the girl tightening, tightening in violet,
Now a soft, salvelike, moth-sheen on her lips—
Hitch up the skeins and the vertical ropes
As if a skeleton hangs, the sky's leech,
And you go dancing, dancing—sunset, dark—
Pouring silver glitter from a top hat.

The Blue Men of the Desert

The blue men of the desert seen through the window of a blue
    room,

Their camels heaped with brilliant rugs, bags, perhaps loaded for
    a wedding—
You do not know if they are leaving or going home.

These wishes come upon you at the edge of things,
The lean, bearded men and the girls with purple lips—
They seem to know exact locations: palms and springs.

Something you wish you knew like truth or paradise—
The world divided by figs, fountains, the stretch of sand,
The slow, bumpy camel-walk, the girl with kohl around her eyes.

You want to know where to set down, pitch tents, light fires.
It is these edges of the flatly real, the rich imagination,
That put the tension tightly in between your percepts and desires.

In fact, outside, not even a playpen full of sand:
The blue room is just a trick of evening—
It is the blurring of the edges that has gotten out of hand.

Still, how stark it is without this other might and magnitude,
Why not be outrageous, call the peacock in to throne you—
Subject to our moods, the map of edges holds but is not glued.

Up to the Hilt

It was a day so brilliant and clear
A spirit-lamp lighted the geraniums.
A swan materialized on the pond
Poured from some blue desire inside you,
An icon floating on a general force.
Think of the shape struggling in your vitals,
Blue light burning all night in your belly,
The retentiveness, the long rubato.

Athletes and soldiers know this: how they must
Hold back their strength until the right moment:
The sudden leap, the battle cry, the shot—
Power held, redoubled, then power spent.

At dawn I saw the water glass turn blue,
Offering its draft of prolongation.
My naked body plated with sunshine,
My own saliva tasting of pep pills.

Just two images spent so far, the swan,
Pure, but lifting his sleek neck like a snake,
The insistent radiance of geraniums.
There was a commando in the garden:
I must stretch out the day to suit his will.
Blue skies would sustain me, ravishing flowers;
The lover would rise in her soft blue gown,
A vestal of vast imagining.

I know that breakfast may buffet, poke us,
A crocodile's jaws grinding the grape nuts,
A matador mired in the marmalade.
Take joy, take strength from the long-withheld,
Wise, willing concierge of consciousness:
The matador cleaned to his suit of lights,
The crocodile sated, faced down by the foil
You plunge in the neck of the raging day.

The Apse in the Afternoon

Two on the beach, an entwined pair.
So much supple bronze and oil,
Neither do they spin, neither do they toil:
He strokes her breast, she runs her fingers through his hair.

Then silent in the sun, posing, dozing, thus,
A double life, a double death—
One cannot discern a single breath
As if two bodies lay atop a modern sarcophagus.

The tidal sea cannot reach their feet,
Gulls fly over, ceremonial—
The sun knows and knows but will not tell
How many times lovers will repeat

An open air cathedral scene
As if they gave up stone, and gave
Not a single thought to lying in a nave—
We have not chosen to belittle or demean

Love that seems so old, yet barely has begun
To think of turning into silent gold,
Arms, legs, turn, infold—
So do they toil? And are they spun?

Darkness comes, a chill cathedral air—
The towel picked up like tapestry, their scattered things,
As if somewhere an angel sings
About this almost forever-imaged pair.

II

White Book

A white book from a foreign land,
Beside it a white sapphire paperweight—
The dangerous know how to do these things.
A ceiling fan turns slowly overhead
Like the ghost of a helicopter
To remind you they will be flying in.
You twitch the curtains—a detective
Standing there on the corner in white light?

You remember her underwear was white,
Silk, lace, draped on the chair by the window,
Left there perhaps as a signal to them.
Her red kisses and blue sapphire bracelet
Did not fool you, nor the smart red herring
Of embraces, romantic overtures—
The lethal drug in her bag, the last drink,
The filching of the book from the table.

All of the evidence stacked against you,
And your strong demands for a day in court—
After much abuse, will they let you go?
A white pill, placebo, to be swallowed
When the woman returns to check on you:
Too much circumstance—this is what you get,
A covert world of uneasy feeling,
The doctor's depressor on a white tongue.

Still there must be a way out of it, an escape—
The blue tie and socks, elegant suede shoes,
The strolling down the street, the rich vitrines,
The still, manic sapphires infused with blue,
The looking back, the fire in the window.
In spite of it all, your best-kept secrets:
Just say, leukemia in remission,
Repealing blue laws as you move along.

The Weight of the Mastiff

These are fast-fading days for castle and chateau:
You send me a postcard, and I send you one,
And, in this way, we collect the world quite on the go.

These postcards are just entries in a far-flung log.
We were there, of course—You gave the beggar a coin,
And I, quite visibly, was bitten by the castle dog.

These are the accoutrements of where we were, and really are.
You come home that much poorer, with no memory of a face,
And no hair of the dog that bit me will quite remove the scar.

We bought the postcards and had the scene, focussed, clear and
    neat.
Who would have thought that beggar would come shambling into
    view,
Or that the snarling dog would look on me as something rather
    good to eat?

The strange, vague thing is that we send our dreams into the air
Without the slightest ballast, burden, a castle on the Rhine, a
    French chateau,
And leave upon the ground the evidence that we were ever there.

This storm of cards rising from that plaintive face, the leg as
    tenderloin!—
Is the vicious dog the only one who really tastes the world?
Did you wait to see what the beggar bought with that extracted
    coin?

Piranha

Put away the sharp letter opener
That has slit the white throats of envelopes.
Hide the pincushion stuck over and over;
Disregard the scimitar on the wall
Which may have designs on the jugular vein,
Pretending only a decorative use.
Still something lethal is circulating
As if a secret wound had motive power.

The goldfish blandly case the sunlit room.
Could they have the teeth of the piranha?—
Happier thoughts glide in on their canoe:
The siesta in the tropics, the hand
Dangled as the suave, harmless fish swim by.
The fingers have an unknown marble life,
Thrust up somewhere, a pedestal of peace—
Never mind that a gold ring went missing.

On the way home, the swaying straphanger
Half dozes among hard looks of mayhem.
Must he always read the news upside down?
Has his small son found the concealed handgun,
That hazy room, those meek fish, a deathtrap?
Someone has to stabilize it somehow—
The canoe keeps pushing on, the white hand
Settles for the safety of ladyfingers.

Don't mind at all that you switch scenes on me—
These competitions go on anywhere:
Dangling hand, tub, and the blood-red water,
Milady putting on her silken gloves.
It is like the unknown in works of art,
The piranha feeding, finding marble,
And gliding on and on the green canoe:
The finger in the bowl thrills or thrashes—
I watch and wonder what you have in mind.

Extraction of Pearls

She does not think of it but pearls are tears
Congealed around the irritation in an oyster's shell—
Who knows how many times it felt tiny panics, little fears?

Beauty hesitates, waits and waits, abides—
We dream and dream, and in the early morning
Feel the milky substance flowing in our sides.

It could be a pebble, grain, that gives, by chance, the start—
How many of us among the closed have pearled and pearled
Because of some deep gravity of heart.

Men and oysters, subtle cousins because long ago they drank
The sea together? Landed, and left behind,
For joint remembrance they have destiny to thank.

The lovely woman fondles, senses, but does not know adventures,
      shared, unsung—
Perhaps one day a callous lover should tell her
Of another wincing when the pearls were pierced and strung.

Should he hesitate or come right out and say, a hint of gallows
In the way the necklace, bright and hard, is hanging,
Why lovers of lustrous beauty have so many cousins and unhappy
      fellows?

Colander

Put yourself in a place where you can do
No wrong, where the soil has been manured
With gold, the sea seeded by sapphire.
The sand shifts topaz through a colander,
But it grates a little on your bottom.
Perhaps the lump sum had a stone in it,
Perhaps the foot undermined by filth,
Cuts and scratches from the blue, glassy sea.

242

Still you persist and hail the paramour:
There are pickups even in paradise.
Lavish the glowing landscape upon her,
Stripped down to nothing but your dangling tie.
Open oysters to make her a necklace,
One she can swallow, one she can gulp down.
It will take you a while to realize
That beauty can sometimes be bagged with pearls.

Now comes the hard part, coarse grains and gravel,
An Idea sat upon a bit too long,
The fertilizer in the rotten fruit,
Entwined bodies, rivulets of sweat,
The soul somehow left in the colander—
I describe the morning of a glutton,
The ravishing lure, the lump in the throat,
The louche lover and orange seeds in the bed.

Still, by the sink, the little holes still hold—
The thick house, the heart wanting to be strained,
That landscape heavy, held, and pouring down,
The rot of things safe, salvaged, and set free—
You are thus assailed in your own kitchen.
Do those holes wink when you pass them?
Lob in the jewels and mash down the chunks:
The hardest look may one day blink you by.

White Lie

Sometimes, if rarely—sometimes only—
We want to say to color: Hush your mouth—
To red in hemorrhage: Give us drouth—
We, for places deep in white, are lonely.

It could be a sculpture garden—
If Ancient Greek, the tincture gone,
Drained without a trace upon the lawn:
Color, going, never asks your pardon.

Through the foramen of Henry Moore,
I see the sky—the blue fights back.
Just wait for night—the moon, not blue, in suave attack
Is looking through Brancusi's spectral door.

Still, in the dark, the statues weep,
Red tears coming in a flood—
So we ask our rich and passionate blood:
White is monumental—but how deep?

Is it too late—the temple, shrine?—
Brancusi, Moore, we pray:
Give us white, white, just for today,
Hiding our lips that mean to call for wine.

III

Expeditions of the Eye

When the eyelash fell, it longed to be a barge—
Stalled in the stagnant water of the eye.
It dreamed stately craft, Cleopatra's ship
Smooth sailing from the dock of the eyelid,
A trace of mascara greasing the hull.
Some such enlargement assails the body,
The pull-away of urgent loneliness
A follicle of folly grown tumid.

Of course, weeping inevitably follows
As the lash passes the eye's waterfall,
The craft sinks like a stone in the harbor.
Cleopatra's silks rise to the bloodshot source,
And the mirror reflects the catastrophe.
You ask: What, who hit you with this hindrance?—
All you wished was a day off from stupor,
Some small part having a day of its own.

Even the slightest breath blows it away,
Gone is the gift of the chasseur of chance.
The lash has gone inward, hoping for pearls:
The maddening irritation, then aground
On the moist rim of a little red beach,
No voyage after all, no pearls, no loot—
She may reach for the fierce eyebrow tweezers:
They at least promise a flotilla.

How close was the lover to this venture?—
His eyelashes brushed her cheek that warm night:
An armada gathered the metaphor,
His folded handkerchief foiled the stranded.
It does not matter if he knew, the sire
Of safe haven—You brush a brown hair
From his shoulders. The table shakes with storm—
The parts of us that coalesce, becalm,
Know that we seethe so that the heart can sail.

Dutch Interior

Sometimes it is the view into the other room that counts—
It is not enough to stand in clear light on polished floors.
Look on, look deep, we say: the interest mounts.

A string of rooms is almost like a game—
It is an accordion pulled out, a pleated music:
Passion, if we have it, insulates within a frame.

The whole house seems hermetic, highly polished—
You might even imagine if you could look outside
A town laid bare, a world demolished.

This is the conceit of counting on recessive steps—
You have a sense of bearing on and boring in:
The light is leading us through vistas opening, concealing depths.

We are hung, of course, with all the riches of each room,
Reflections from mirrors, a mistress on each arm:
I am lugging Cupid's blindfold statue—What next?—the wings of
    Mercury, the zoom?

No, not quite. But anything so closed is retreating from retreat:
The shining tiles are like a chessboard, the game is always on:
Slip a little, slide a little, recidivist of sight, move on into the dark,
    but watch your feet.

The Hairbrush

Turned over, stuffed with hair, it could remind
You of a clogged sink that grew too ambitious,
Tried to swallow a head—a bad day that!—
But something ripples in the room and rights
The oval, the handle—Could it have started
Life as a tadpole, also ambitious,
Overweening, scuttling along the sand,
A bristled creature with a carapace—

A handsome silver horseshoe crab at last.
A jogger on the beach might pick it up,
Ruminate and ruminate the silver
As he saw it on his lover's dresser,
Remembering the inveigled hairs like strings
Of a harp, the strangled, hidden music,
How a fetish lives in a single word,
And will accost you again and again.

It can be a hairraising experience
To let go altogether and feel the edges
Of the known world tremble and long to be
Volcanic, the brush like a burning ghost:
The silence and the petrified object.
Your house and mine are full of them, the things
That nothing but the mind can animate,
The secret scuttling along the sea bed.

One could go on and on—the protuberant
Pedal of the piano, modest, lowly,
But lyric to the large body of sound.
I do not wish to harangue Harlequin
To come, let down his hair in the moonlight:
The long lustrous sheen hostile to crewcuts,
Stubbled deserts—that is for another time—
I pluck a single hair and play our song.

The Camera and the Keyboard

Now that you have limbered up your fingers,
You can play the day any way you like—
A sentimental little tune or one that lingers.

At your fingertips, power, passion, everything you know:
Sunrise, sunset, a song of sexual satisfaction—
Some say they are a camera, you are a piano.

For you do not want the picture, snapped and still—
You want it to flow, flourish, down the river,
Over the waterfall, if it must, and spill.

Rest, of course, a moment when you spatter—
The fumes of white withdrawn around a pool,
A golden glow, a girl bathing in the water.

So you wanted after all a holding, an effect
Of fingers lifting from the cosmic keyboard
To curl and reach around the naked shoulders of a subject.

The long, ecstatic flowing, the glimmering stasis holding back—
You see yourself kissing her, holding on as if forever,
And there, above, the furious water cutting you some slack.

The Camel That Broke the Back of the Straw

His limber spine was like a golden stalk,
And the great foot was coming down on it,
The huge mass of the beast, the wide desert,
The saddlebags filled with exotica.
Could he really bear even one more day—
The swaying, hairy beast in his bedroom
Where he himself had stepped on many bones,
The lovers that went like straws in the wind?

They come upon us, these reverse meanings—
Some mornings flat in bed, the lifted foot,

The fragrant mattress a dusty straw tick:
You lie on the rough passions of the world,
The last lover and the final pressure.
Can you remember her long, slave-girl look,
How it seemed that your hands had turned to feet,
The spring's crushed air of daffodils, mustard?

Should you arch it one more time for others,
The back like a beckoning Bridge of Sighs?—
Dreaming of love's soaring, supple rainbow,
Shouldering at least a sensual peacock,
Iridescent underwear and blue desire—
Strong enough to be walked all over,
Saddled with briefcases of bright feathers,
The tall beast and the forever-bearing:

Or close on that prostrate nude in the sand?
The oncoming and implacable mass,
The trampled torso, the eyes squashed like grapes,
Better to wake, a glass straw in the mouth,
Orange juice rather than a camel's kumiss,
The clinical white, the claustral comfort—
Who knows whether the book with a broken back
Still holds the spine of a peacock feather?

Zipper

You pull the tab, the slinky dress drops down,
She pulls it up your fly, and says: "No thanks."
Closets of unzipped clothes show small, blunt teeth:
The whole world is a maw of mixed motives.
Sometimes a harmony in the clenched groove,
The perfect back, the perfect bulge revealed:
This is the time when wounds are winning streaks—
The lips of the universe are open.

Still, mishaps plague the lilting microcosm,
Stuck half way, you need a pair of pliers,
A contretemps not easily concealed—

Who wants to walk around with such a tool
Stashed in the pocket for emergencies?
Would one call the management, or just pause,
Glare at the details of desuetude,
Swear you hear the other garments laughing?

Those open mouths, those gullets, those filed teeth,
Cannibals with their clothes in the closets—
So you went too fast, the road sinuous,
Perhaps you stalled just short of a steep cliff.
Now the tab feels like a little road sign
That was coming down with you all the time,
The blind eyesocket aimlessly fingered,
A tassel of danger on smooth tarmac.

Back home, you lie naked in the moonlight
Except for a jockstrap which will not slide,
Dreaming the long odysseys of zippers:
Filmy nightgowns never touched by metal,
Curving roads that end in flowered meadows—
You cannot help but mix and split the two.
The nightmare may be the black, zipped-up zebra,
Too tight to ever show white stripes again.

The Double Bed

Looking back at the sun's iridescence
From the fanlight in the hall, he should have
Known that a spectacle lay ahead,
A sense that life's passion still propelled him.
But how could he have guessed that someone had
Let the preposterous bird in from the garden,
That icon of his sensual adventures,
The sparrow he had coaxed into full glow?

Still, he was not at all prepared to see
The peacock on the bed, his tail spread out,
A dazzling counterpane, all eyes on him,
The multiple vision, his own voyeur—

The one prodded by the light toward ecstasy.
You can say that it is only sunspots:
Rub your eyes—the white coverlet is bare,
A vanished sludge of blue, purple, and gold.

Nevertheless, you will never forget
The way the mind can take off down the hall
In the sunlight, in groomed luxuriance,
As if you picked pictures out of the dust,
The orgasm of the opening door—
That last look at the bruise on your white hand
As if you came to blows to come to this,
An indigo imprint from the bouncer.

Pushed from many rooms, you have persisted,
The surge of language as the doorknob turned,
The bright blue porcelain in a stranglehold.
Just so, the gorge rises in the white throat.
You relax, and you are free to report
The peacock in its very latest pose.
Lie down, lover, lie down with me in my mind,
And let the sunlight cover us with eyes.

The Eye of the Beholder

There was, after all, a throb in the day:
Perhaps just a lance-like look at the sea,
And you feel blue has hit you in the heart—
The minuscule on the sand a lost lover?
The telescope and her sad, piquant smile.
This longing to bring back, bring close, bring in:
The sun staking your shadow on the wall,
The ring on her hand flashing an omen.

The room, of course, is only a junk heap:
Tangled sheets, clothes, food on the floor, a shoe
Unreachable, maddening, under the bed
That says try if you will to go anywhere.
Leaning towers of dishes in the kitchen sink

Will crash if you pass them in stocking feet—
That sea, then, why that banderilla of blue,
Why that girl smiling in a silent film?

It will come back to you that yesterday
Is like an animal being taunted—
Turned on by a kiss that still could be yours,
Today, the oldest of all temptations.
The lance wants an athlete on its sharp point,
The telescope would die for a true tear—
Crocodiles asleep in a flooded basement,
The swamp where smiling lovers broke their vows.

The world keeps dealing in sharp practices:
The bull in the mirror takes one more thrust,
The athlete escapes in his suit of lights,
Finds his cape in the girl's spread-out beach towel.
It is too late not to believe in anything.
The tower takes another dish—sunlight,
Stabbing, holds its hands for just that moment
When you lie stuck together on the sand.

Medieval Moments

In October you are still half-summer-young, not yet old—
It is time to refill the coffers before more hours are spent:
Enrich, enrich—the air itself breathes gold.

It is the right occasion for artisan's aplomb—
You can feel the body filling up with ore,
And lie stretched out on your bed as on a tomb.

Perhaps one day you will have a place in some cathedral,
A corner, brilliant, lit, where bees can buzz
As if they came from everywhere to tend an icon of the fall.

This filling, carving process, this sense of matrix:
For an hour or two one does not even have to contemplate
That everything in life depends upon specifics.

252

It is wonderful to think a dream can last for ages,
But the heavy book keeps turning, turning,
And men, like flowers, are pressed between the pages.

Let mine be saturate with pollen like goldenrod—
If not stone or metal, at least immortal print,
Specific as to how face, arms, body looked, and how the feet were
    shod.

IV

Zodiac Arrest

The sorrow of not hitting the bull's-eye,
That icon, that red image of the sun,
Like a wall painting in the open air:
Then the mortification of falling
Outside the tense planetary circles—
If you can't hug the sun, go hissing out
Into space, the junk-heap of broken shafts:
The Archer has done what he can for you.

This is for those who have felt the plucked twang
Over and over, and yet missed the mark:
That fellow sharp as an arrow—poets
Who have ravished the lyre for better strings,
Hearing the same discord, only lonelier,
The heart marked forever with lost wedges,
The cuneiform of derivation:
The Word, the moving target of the sun.

Lovers, most of all, know the wayward aim,
Wanting to shoot for the stars, a firm place
Beside Sagittarius, willing to be
Split down the middle, to let the passage
Through, but mainly settling for the pubic wound—
The deep, treacherous gut has lost its chance,
The body feels hunchbacked as the bent bow:
Androgynous Eros, a rouged tart.

Nevertheless, again and again, somehow
We put ourselves into the shafting mode,
Interchangeably, archer and arrow,
Hoping that dual roles can agitate
The universe—the arrow pulling the man.
One lies apart at night fingering sex—
Why was the wound so shallow, so sharp?
She turns her lips for me to touch their bow.

Anatomy of Scars

You must pull out the arrow and then the thorn
If you want your dreams to flourish and expand:
Frangipanni, blue dawns, bronzed girls for which you think that
    you were born.

You were not meant to be a martyr or a saint.
Not even Sebastian, the arrows and that cruel glamour:
Your skin, if you still go on dreaming, wants no prick, no bruise,
    no taint.

Remember the piercing, piercing love that so appealed?—
When it was withdrawn, the words, the kisses, taken back,
You met the next girl naked in the sun and healed.

It taught you that the world keeps bearing down, buffeting,
    looming,
You must oil yourself with every tropic dream you can—
Even the savages and their hail of arrows are dazzled by your
    clever way with grooming.

Still positioned near that phallic palm, the blue, voluptuous
    lagoon,
Some ill-forgotten love keeps working in your side—
Blessed twilight comes, but there is blood upon the moon.

Will she be coming back, ever young and beautiful
To gloss the bruise, the gimlet marks, fondle where the pain is,
Find the deep, discounted point of it, and pull?

Family Reunion

The corn is the cousin of the callus
Once removed, born of tight shoes, loose
Lives perhaps that love dancing until dawn,
Standing at the bar, one more for the road,
Home with the hangover, the hot footbath,
But maybe, just maybe, it grows by stealth
While you stay home reading a book of poems,
Some frozen music in a faulty vein.

The callus is more sure of heritage—
It has known the carcass for a lifetime:
The heavy treading, endless balance act
As if it can feel the planet turn—
Violence, vice—tiptoe to the keyhole,
Kick the door in if the lover has lied.
The cold floor and the sizzling hot pavement—
Wouldn't you want to walk on tough shields if you could?

So you have comforts no cousin has,
In a pinch, walk on broken glass, embers—
While you lie dozing, safe from a spoiled child,
Prankish with a pin, a future footpad.
Still that lucky corn begins the beguine,
Those hot, tight shoes a kind of testament:
Nothing so far has worn you to the bone,
Your priest of pedicare, good Doctor Scholl.

The golden apples of Atalanta
May be strewn by some man not fleet of foot,
Or a jogger trade you for a blister.
Love the beautiful, worship brave, deft feet,
A myth stamped hard on the side of your toe—
Family reunions of corn and callus.
Leave it to heaven, bare, unblemished soles:
After all those miles, tenderfoot again.

The Fever Blister

Was it turbulence of mind and heart or just the thing he ate?—
Homunculus, little monkey, feeding on bananas and bad faith,
The Braille of a devious tumor has something to communicate.

It is the end of the line, terminal moraine, the kiss-off, Mister.
Whether you dine on somebody else's hope, haggis, hors
    d'oeuvres, a little histrionic,
Can you say for sure that it was one, the other, both combined, that
    made the blister?

Late at night, succeeding an enormous and insulting meal,
A drunken friend calls, talks endlessly about the sorrows of the
    world—
Though you are numb, narcotized, the tissue of your orifice will
    feel.

Inter alia, life is passions, pillow fights, poetry, hives—
The skin of your lips is left long after the skin of your teeth
Has gone the sad, sad way of bad investments and lost wives.

Just when you have another date or dinner coming up—no place
    to hide—
The pustule puts a touch of Dorian Gray upon your mouth.
Pointing to the place where paté, pique, patently elide.

I have a very rueful feeling as the years go by—
I must label japes and jars of caviar with caveats
And caution every moral rising to the lips: You might have been a
    stye,

The Window Doctor

What gave him the idea the sea was ill,
That his view of it needed a deft touch,
Even a drop, a spoon, of blue medicine,
That it called to him for bedside manner.

His own fine-tooth comb was full of gold hairs,
He flaked and flaked from so much harsh sunshine,
Wanted the bluest salve to heal his wounds.
All he had left was this narrow sea-slit,
The whole body like a hot eye glaring.
Tossed there by the retching of the waves,
Sun-tanned swimmers lay entangled on the beach.
A man in a wetsuit holding a spear
Looks like a devil with a golden head:
No flakes at night when he will rubber off,
No gold strands in the comb for sorrow's harp—
These visions assail you at the window.
So the blue world is there to be treated.
A gull has the wings of a nurse's cap.
The skin diver will lend you his scalpel,
The telephone rings, and you are on call.
It will take all of your tact and tenderness,
The whole bag of tricks in the instrument kit,
To recoup your brilliant way with the sea:
The first time you saw it in glorious health
When it said "Ah," and you smelled its fresh breath,
Your hand on the belly quivered with pleasure.
No wonder your lover hung blue curtains,
Placed the cool aquamarine next to your skin
As if she knew your need of a compress.
Juice, jam, rolls, coffee—the blessed morning—
It is time to remove the bandages.
Stand at attention in your whitest suit—
The sea is holding out its bright blue tongue:
I see the shuttered window blinking tears.

V

April Sunshine

Two cats are in a window in a sunny spot—
Are they lovers? Brothers? Sisters? On such a beautiful day
Does it really matter: Which is? What not?

Does it matter if one cat is yours, one mine
As animals seem to favor master, mistress?—
We are all enclosed in a dream of April sunshine.

Beyond the window, a mélange of spring:
Jonquils, hyacinths, tulips, all so fresh—
We are naked in the room, light is lavish, and we are drinking,

Just as the cats are taking in their sunshine sop.
There must be a glorious world of water beneath this ground:
We do not ever want the pouring down of sunshine, the welling up
    to stop.

The constant worry of whether I belong to you, you to me,
Will a catfight break out in another hour,
Are just as improbable as that water, rising high, will become a sea.

If so, we cling and cling together on the highest spot, the trees, the
    Judas smoke,
Purplish-pink—and we will see at last the vapor of our vast
    desire—
Cats and lovers, keeping heads just above their ecstasy, swimming
    on and on together, stroke by stroke.

Wild Onions

In every encounter they had the sense
Of the peeler, just the mere taking off
Of their clothes, her fruitlike, orange chiffon,
His brown and white like potato parings.
Was it just an old Edenic impulse
That their clothes had grown on them too closely,
That they put on another rind each day?—
Her rich hat itself supported a garden.

So there it was at last, the basic skin,
And still the wish to put a knife to it,
Round and round, the deep, unraveling love—
Her breast, sweet, heaped-up, high-banked, fungoid.
His chest an undevastated undergrowth,
The mattress itself lumpy with spring bulbs:
The closets and drawers loaded with layers,
Discarded, resumed, discarded, resumed.

Dressed in the steeped kitchen, one remembers
Peeling onions, the stinging eyes, the tears,
The same odor, the fast-dwindling mass,
And wondering if it were all worth it,
As if human figures were wild onions,
As if lying in bed were a furrow,
And the sad desire to get to the heart
Of things left tears, ineradicable odor.

Comes night again, the crescent moon offers
Us its high, cold, ironic scythe to cut
Us down to size if we go wandering:
The spicy, musky odor everywhere,
His strong, curved hand, her smaller, defter one—
The bulbs stir uneasily beneath them
As if, mulched and mulched in metaphysics,
The deepest paradox is being skinned alive.

Fairweather Friends

So your toucan does not like you anymore—
Did it see you make glorious love last night,
And say to itself at dawn: This one plans to show me the door.

You should have had sense enough to put the cloth over the cage:
The violet-eyed beauty, those kisses, those penetrations—
Enough to dizzy anyone with envy, and then enrage.

Offer fruit this morning—the toucan takes your finger.
You try to pull away, but those large, turned down shears
Take their own sweet time, and linger.

It is too bad, you were such golden friends,
Making eye-love, preening, touching lips and beak—
Now the only solution—get rid of the violet girl and make amends.

The world stretches us like this so many ways—
If not a bird, a peeper at the window:
Looking in on others is a field so many want to graze.

Of course, of course, you should have found your bird a mate,
Then no end of violet girls, kissing, cooing, preening, treading—
Love is a violent, crowded place, and no one wants the gate.

Close Quarters

If handling too much, too carelessly, you
Get a powder burn, take blue from the sea,
The liquid unguent that leaves you free—dust
From a moth's wings perhaps, the cool, dipped rose
With its soft flagellation of romance:
The belief that the handled woman too
May have seen the flash of the gun nearby,
A smell in the air of smoking metal.
Somewhere a peacock is shaking down its spots
Just in case you need another mixture.

A lipstick fallen in the dewy grass
Recalls her need for your assistance;
A slightly burned man may have a soothing touch,
His scars touched up with blue and silver salve
Made up from the fine-ground eyes of the bird.
The closeness that almost kills also cures—
She is pulling you into her again with pearls.
Look: She is hung with silken halters,
Not too much shaken by the sudden shot.
Let her jars of moth dust cake a little,
Her own emollient wait for your label—
After the powder burn, these gifted dreams.
Of course, this story of close range requires
An abiding passion for gun control.
The woman has every right to believe
That the retrieved lipstick in your pocket
Turns in the old specific, red spiral.
It is the jam-packed life she wants from you.

Killer Bees

If nothing around you seems to please—
Beautiful women bore, the wine acid, the fruit rotten at the core—
Count your blessings that, so far, no killer bees.

Lips that used to stimulate now taste bland,
Wine is blue and bilious as blood from a tired vein:
Drop that spotted fruit at once. Don't even smell your hand.

Stars that always stabbed you with desire
As your arm tightened around the scented and enfabled waist,
Say time to go to bed, old boy. Put out the fire.

The unwelcome sword that morning flashes in your eyes
Calls up those images of dashing men and duels
Only to ream and ream around the room and cut you down to size.

This is when you thank those cold, unlucky stars: No hum—
A sense of some vast hostility at the open garden gate,
Ready to fit a buzzing mask upon the man you have become.

Masque of the Red Death? Black the dominant color of alarm?
Kiss the woman one more glorious time. Drink wine. Eat fruit—
Is that a fluttering shadow on the window of some all-expansive
    swarm?

Geisha

I remember her painted cheeks and hair dark as a crow's wing—
As she moved, sat in her elaborate kimono playing the samisen,
It was as though a whole embroidered country had learned to
    dance and sing.

I stay at home, I do not travel much, at least not anymore—
Therefore the geisha, perfumed, packed with so much art and
    grace,
Seems to subtly close the world around me and then fling wide the
    door.

For there the willow wavers and the country wanders on her robe,
And when she extends in her white hands a cup of tea,
It is as if she held, held back a while, a reproduction of the globe.

There is a peaceful lake somewhere along the silk—No doubt
The eye would find it if it searched a sensual moment more:
We would stay, spend the afternoon and night closing in and
    opening out.

Morning comes, my bags are packed, and I, once more, am on the
    go—
I have a garden world to live, a lake to find:
Great travels have indeed been launched by nothing but a cup of
    tea.

The Blue Line

He came on board without a reservation—
This man with his tongue purple-coated
As if he had licked the bloom from the grapes
Or marinated his palate in wine,
Inhaled draughts of iris the long spring through—
He is ready to dance a blue tango, or play
In a combo his dusky, twilight music.
Mignonne, it matters, it matters indeed,
That you wear a blue dress to suit his mood,
That ripe plums are piled on the rich sideboard,
That you also believe in a moment of truth,
That if you start here you will arrive there:
The space between you somehow will be filled,
The right turn in the tango, the licked grape,
The swallowed dust, and the remembered spring.
It is the localizing of life that counts,
These thick concentrates, these partners in blue.
One cannot keep the mouth full forever,
Or the poison mounts, the one dose too much,
And the lapis will leach on the blank floor.
But I have eaten grapes, with friends, lovers,
And let the world's misprision, for a time,
Look in wonder on an exaltation.

VI

The Jogger by the Sea

The gray day when brilliance, light, were needed,
You said: I am the jogger by the sea,
So lithe, so evenly tanned, so perfect
As if washed all over by spot remover,
Leaving just the hard, metallic finish.
It was the sun coming out in the man,
Concentrating the hidden thing in the sky.
It is this desire to break through, burnish,
Which fuels the spirit-lamp in the heart,
Moves the jogger against the cold, raw wind
As you plunge a warm finger in a glove,
As you stand by the dead fire like fuel.
The jogger always wears red for tinder,
Hiding the bagged secrets of a lifetime.
The driftwood ignites when he passes by,
The sea smokes and wants to boil over blue
It is this great fullness one wants to foist,
Loping along a most uncertain coast,
The car lights across the road like grotesque eyes,
Others abroad, prowling the misty day.
An accident is a distinct possibility:
Life is so easily flung on the ground.
Therefore, those running shorts in your bureau
Lie like acid among pale underwear.
They too were dipped, deeply dipped, and then dried,
The next time you take them out, look in the mirror,

Examine every inch of your skin for tan:
Is this the day to penetrate the fog?
Is this the day of days loaded within you,
Sun-packed by your long saga with desire?—
But just be careful of the overlooked,
The place on the heel life held you by
Where the spot remover could never reach,
The white wound bequeathed by all our mothers.
Like Achilles, upside down, the jogger
Must blink the coming fear of sunless days.

Tell Us, Tarantula

I have known it before, beside the purple mountains and blue
    sea—
The youthful skin was bronze and quite invulnerable,
Teleology meant nothing in the world except: To be.

Of course, too long, too long, and something in the sun began to
    boil—
The hairy spider seemed to smell a passion in the air,
Or could he see a savage touch of color iridescent in the oil?

One thinks of these transitions, how we lure the sting and proffer
    balm—
Something is taking place in that clear light, in that clear mind:
Amber dropped around the spider like a scarab caught beneath
    the palm.

Something paused, pondered—you can feel the feelers—would
    they pierce and bore?—
Curious how you are still the shining prince touched up with color,
And never meant to be to that tarantula a toreador.

The luscious, brilliant, and this somewhat leaner, land—
One wears the suit of lights, more red and weathered now:
I feint, and do not faint to see a drop of blood upon the sand.

266

Tarantula from *tableau vivant*—ecstasy, uncased, and breaking free
    from amber—
I see a power come to term, I see it crossing over,
And fling myself ecstatic in the sun each time that I remember.

Magnifying Glass

You lift, lower, move it from side to side,
For you know that if the eye fell, it would
Be a hard trampoline, more like a pond
Of ice where sight slips to oblivion,
See-through ice so that you saw death's figure
As the last thing before you reached the brim.
Still, you are in control, you lift the lens,
And a large, pleasant vagueness fills the air.

One needs a steady hand, up, down, back, forth—
What should be enlarged, what should be kept blurred?
The swimmer in the eye wants a soft plunge,
The skater to move on and on forever,
So the hand has been schooled in compromise
Though the eye still lusts for the blue trampoline
That will return it to the diving board,
Happy recidivist, gilded by the sun.

But the accolade goes to the skater
Who knows that figures move beneath the ice,
Loves the peering face, the positive pounce
As though a word slipped, fell, must be rescued,
Set back on its feet, a crystal icon.
Still, the little swimmer will crowd the act
At the least chance to show yielding depth,
The drenched playback of high passion.

Sometimes the glass is surfeited with words:
Such manic playmates over and over,
A cracked skull, a crushed, bleeding, golden bird,
The high, low, world, a junk of junctures.
I have seen men and myself raise the glass

As if sieving the air for cosmic dust.
What can be collected in a lifetime:
Swimmers, skaters, secret traces, shedding stars?

The Quill

Into the mess of things—this too shall pass?
A crow's feather falls as from violent foray:
If life has nothing else, it has accumulation, mass.

I picked it up, held it for a moment, iridescent, still—
Useless in my hand, but skilled and beautiful in flight:
Too late for bonnet or for quill.

What is this unconquerable obsession to dwell
On things that merely happen, fall without import?—
At this moment into the congeries a feather fell.

The warrior, the purple ink, the writing table, rise,
The bonny soldier prince, the dipper, the glorious dabbler,
Up from the solid mess of things before my eyes.

Well, we think, perhaps, why not hang on a while?—
The fallout from combat and flight may be another iridescence:
Fantasies and figures pull up their bootstraps from the pile.

I brought the feather in, and laid it by my pen—
Nothing happened, no glistening burst, no rallying, no rout either:
The enormous, growing mass—a breeze, a flutter. And then? And
    then.

Clam

On some seashores the sands are mined with them—
Men of imagination walk softly,

Otherwise you go in with a pronged fork
When the ocean's armament is rolled back,
Bent over, looting the deserted land:
Here a flat flint stone, there the head of an axe
Left from the wars of the waves. But who cares?—
Hunger ordains the moratorium.

Still one learns a little from everything:
A flair for the messages of mollusks—
The digger himself, a tense, tight-lipped man,
Filled with stalled tears, the soft meat of sorrow.
Don't say too much anytime, anywhere,
The tumult returns, and you will be tossed.
Someone will try to pry you wide open
With the knife of a sharp, savage remark.

The man of imagination roams, always roams,
Sees the tight-closed thing metastasize,
Become the giant clam shell from the South Seas,
Monster teeth mimicking the little rake,
Grabbing the thin leg of the pearl diver
As if luxury lured the cannibal.
I am told the flesh is purple as the sash
Of a pirate: the diver, sabered, savored.

Back home, the dunes, the hard inland domain—
The gangling go-getters, garrulous mouths,
The ruthless and the simply dim-witted
Cannot abide the quiet, the clammed-up,
Who dine with deep sea cannibals in secret,
Regurgitate the diver in their dreams.
Beware, beware, pirates of privacy:
A hidden cutlass, and a throat is cut.

Moroccan Magniloquence

It was a winter day, a tangerine from Tangier
Sat on a table, the white cloth like glittering sand,
And seemed to say: "Let me make one thing clear. . . ."

The blue sea and the city rose around it white as chalk—
The tangerine continued its vocalise, "Let me make it perfectly
    clear"—
Whoever would have thought a fruit could talk.

"Let me say once more in a city of little rain,
You will learn the extreme clarities of life:
The kiss gives pleasure, and the knife gives pain.

"In this white room we put so many things to test—
It is the closed oasis of the inordinate:
The clothed and the unclothed, the knife upraised and the naked
    breast."

What could I do to stop the luscious and loquacious mouth?
This beauty and barbarism in abundant tandem?—
I must learn the secret, vast liquidities of drouth.

Keep it a private passion, the haranguing fruit, that you were
    spoken to—
Fountains will gush on the tongue from just one thing deeply
    heard,
Or so a tangerine convinced me that cloth was sand, the sea I could
    not see was blue.

The Tongue

It rarely sleeps, prowling the white-boned cave
All day long, feeling fillings like geodes,
Shaped like a cobra's head with a frenum.
But it can work wonders on a short leash,
Darting, French-kissing, pushing at white gates,
But, most of all, conspiring with the lips
And vocal cords to throw the book at us:
The dictionary, the land of dried tongues.

Still, the main appeal is serpentine—
Some wine-red, others pale as morning light
As if an exoskeleton were shed:

270

The furry-coated thing the doctor sees
Grown wise in the ways of the depressor—
Sick or well, back home the brain can worry
If the roof below may be too weak, thin,
A ceiling unsafe for heaviest thought.

But the tongue is also a slick wizard,
Becomes a slide for food, water and wine,
Counting on room in a lake of lipids,
To those with a stomach ache the dank, deep place
Where Charon plies his dark and mournful trade.
So we spend our lives, tasting, testing, snake,
An atavistic fear of swallowing it.
Glorious, unchoked morning, the captive—

The sigma safe, supple in saliva.
Nothing else so deft and omnipresent,
Ready for rapid words, ululation
As if its guile were borrowed from the wolf.
But at century's end, wishful wanderer,
Torn out by the terrorist, it coils the Tree
Of Life, back in some old, forgotten cave,
The hidden encapsulated Eden:
First man, woman, truth, lies again, revenge.

The Hunt for the Great Blue

He felt hemmed in by the thick blue river,
The banks heavy with iris. Was it sink
Or swim, climb or be cloistered by flowers?—
Found one day, a faded sapphire figure
By the truffle hounds from the fields above,
Snuffed out like a rhizome of rich desire,
The man who could not go either way,
To whom impasse was the last impetus.
One way the river, turn, the iris wall,
A catwalk of closest calibrations,
The little beach, in fact, a tiny breach.
He must dive, walk, climb, unprecedented—

Never the water so deep, so daunting,
Never the iris pressing their tattoos
As if one birthmark were never enough.
If it is too much to ask for blue fish
In the mouth as one rises to the bait,
Reach for the lover in a thicket spelling out
Body art from a lexicon of lust.
You have opened the way like a fresh wound,
The blue, enpurpled blood flowing through the brain.
You can walk on, followed by cicatrix,
The tight scar lipped with water, kissed by flowers,
The hot soles of your feet seaming, seaming.
So enough perhaps for another day:
A line of spirit, a purple passage
Such as things specific cannot disclaim.
It is so close, so close, so caught, confined,
This smell, this smirch, this deep touch of living.

View from a Passion for Phlox

In June the phlox are heating up their spires
Like mushroom towers with look-outs, luxurious restaurants on
    top:
One can see for miles around, and, in another county, forest fires.

This is how, this brilliant day, you choose to loom—
The pink, the purple, and the cool, restraining white
Are called upon to give the mind overreaching room.

Nothing can persuade you to give up, desist, or stop—
The flower grows, enlarges by absolute command
Because you feel yourself, this lucid day, swollen at the top.

The head goes looking far beyond the wall,
Having fed itself upon itself in many summit hours:
I saw the fire, I saw the famous city burn beyond recall.

Come home again, come home to soothing, dulcet white—
The towers are collapsible, the restaurants are closed:
An elevator of relief brings you down at night.

Some loss of appetite perhaps, some scorch-marks on the hands—
It was a day of looking up and looking on and looking over:
We live in the largest, most distant places, and in the common
    lands.

Undine

When the blue wave rose to the swimmer's lips,
It seemed the sea was pleading for his touch:
The encircling arms, the tang of the kiss,
The salt and sapphire of crushing jewels,
A blue lanugo streaming on the skin
As though a child were born in the transfer
And love were lavish with its afterbirth.
So, an ordinary swimmer by the sea
Waits for some marvelous marriage,
While the rising waves heap up their harem:
The soul given, the child, the youth returned—
A man standing in the sun drying off:
No blue hair dangling on the towel, no dropped jewel.
Shall we waive the complicated corollaries?—
The glass of water turning green in the hand,
A godchild babbling in the pocket change,
Even the blown leaves lifting up their lips,
An eye in a ring, the water sprinkler
Shaking us with its too effusive tears,
At sunset, the vast and pregnant mountain.
It is not easy to relate what happened,
But meeting for cocktails at the blue hour,
I find her lovely arms implacable—
What is radiance but this secret child,
The kiss in the dark I summon from the sea?

Man in the Middle of His Images

The leaves have spent so long just being leaves,
But now, as if a dying swan inspired them,
They lend themselves to anything or anyone who grieves.

The swan is far off somewhere in a pond, alone,
But seems to hear the rustling, falling leaves,
And wants to give to them his final, personal tone.

How on earth except in such declining weather
Can swan, leaf, be juxtaposed and blent?—
It takes a human being, fallen too, bringing them together.

It needs a person cognizant of hates, harms,
And disappointed love to make such strange alliances conjoin:
November mixed with memories of Pavlova's fluttering arms.

The swan becomes human, the swirling leaves a ghost,
And you must take this image, that image, this image, that image,
      by the throat
To see how much it still has left of something you have lost.

And then the great, exhausted, lovable release—
The heart is ready for its coverlet of leaves and down of feathers,
Content that summer comes again with fat green leaves and
      waddling geese.

The Work of the Sun

I

Fallen Arches

The feet were so flat not even an ant
Could crawl under them. The mole moving below
Might think there was soft, fleshy ground above,
And push upward, giving momentary support.
One more step—it goes back thousands of years
To sandals, Roman soldiers, the footrace
At Olympia, bruising rocks, the sag
Down the centuries to the stretched, broken span.

But some of us escape time, history:
The swimmer with his supple, gold-lined poise,
The skater spreadeagled on just one leg,
The football player's dropkick near game's end,
His light arms flung out like a butterfly,
The sweating oarsman pushing in the scull,
Blue with desire under the arching bridge:
You, I, alas, not those whom fortune loves.

Still, the world walks forward on faulty feet,
The legs shaky columns, the body
A lopsided architrave that bears the years,
The belly a belvedere, the pendant
Sex a ball longing to ring, raise love's troops—
So the feet in damp socks, tight armor,
Would shed everything; to race Atalanta,
Stones like gold, strewn apples diverting death.

The tired foot sleeps bare, snuggles the lover
Whose instep receives, a cove of comfort:
Half a bridge, half a span, better than none.
The sun calls, Arches of the world: Arise!
If we must philosophize, feet, aroused,
Are the place to start—the blue river calls,
The years shake down some weight like building blocks:
Modest mason, why not vaults and rainbows?

The Navel Gazer

Should one speak at all, comment, make signs?—
The beetroot on the table, the orange, banana,
The sapphire, like a pebble from the sea, buried in the mines.

Is it enough some days just to contemplate
The beets like fallen Russian domes, the orange a shrunken sun,
    the banana's capsized boat?—
Take your time: We become the thing we eat and ate.

Some days should be full of image-pauses.
What caused the towers to fall, the fruit to shrink, the boat
    sprawled on its side?—
One single sentence demands so many clauses.

I sit naked in the sun full of just such leisure,
Remembering how the sea coughed up its pebble, the slashed red
    architecture,
How the swallowed yellow boat was meant to be a cruise of
    pleasure.

Just sit in the sun, let the pauses and the pictures brim—
The beet becomes borsch, the stone a ring, the fruit
    a wrecked and wrinkled skin
Full, full, just so full, no slopping at the rim.

Oh, you will be voluble again tomorrow—
The words will take the lash, cry out like galley slaves.
Dancing on deck, leaping from the bow, flashing rings
    —Inland, the Word is hiding in a barrow.

Hourglass

Few use them anymore, but it seldom
Fails, and is thus incontrovertible.
One could wish it had larger ambitions
And that the sand of the beach could measure
The violent, voluptuous blue ocean,
Straining an element's vast intentions:
A primal timepiece that picks up on shipwrecks,
Lost cargo, drowned swimmers, approaching storms.

But its claims are much more homely, modest,
Eating, regurgitating a single hour,
Less insistent than the ravenous clock
That slices its fine segments endlessly
As if time could provoke indigestion.
There is something suave and smooth in glass,
Stressing the demulcent nature of sand,
One small grain at a time without grievance.

Yet hints of medieval torture
Rise from the lopped head and the quartered limbs,
A woman perhaps, cinctured, wasp-waisted,
Who still ghosts the telling passage of time:
How long till the next blow, meager meal?—
Sunny in the window, the recusant
Has forgotten, forgiven the sinner,
The blood, bruise, oaths, sieved and stored elsewhere.

Now it is fun to come back in an hour,
Turn time on its head like a little clown,
Pinched and held in a tight situation.
It is the grace of the thing that matters,
Telling us oh so mildly we grow old,
Have avoided for now whip and dungeon,
If the kettle boils over, we can thank
Our lucky stars we did not time the ocean.

The Luge

Nothing is more devious than fear—
It can come upon you in a mountain pass,
Without warning, crossing a crevasse,
Or sliding on a small toboggan in your ear.

Perhaps, the least, the most, when all is said—
You cannot easily direct the chute,
No hooks except the foot and boot—
Quite simply, at the end, a hole in the head.

Packed ice, tight banks, a glimpse of trees—
That is what happens when you hear harsh sound,
Something rushing past from higher ground,
A sled of syllables that does not mean to please.

Of course, music has another way:
The waltz, the march, the drum,
Hardly any compositions come
Down in sleds, they commandeer the sleigh.

Tinnitus scores the harmony with error—
I saw a man examining his ear
As if the unexpected runaway were fear:
The schuss, the shout, the crashing in the mirror.

Words, music, moving faster than you think—
You swerve, barely missing that black boulder
When someone taps you on the shoulder:
A spiral spilling from his voice may bring you to the brink.

The Wheatfield

The wheatfield becomes a surge of interest,
The existentialist in you excited,
Waving gold and brown to the horizon
As if it had laid on that blue itself,

The sensuous brush between heaven and earth.
It reminds you of childhood untrammeled:
This way, that way, of a fingerpainting,
The wind helping with your deepest secret.

Even so, civilization at your back,
You must think at least of the swinging scythe,
Back and forth, back and forth, a harder dream:
The cities founded on the craving mouth,
The haystacks mounting like lush golden breasts—
This dream before the dream of the machine,
All interest and desire cooperative,
All childish things gone with the pleasant wind.

Still, you fumble in your damp, dark pocket
For a jacknife, wanting and not wanting,
Needing and not needing, eager to live
And yet leave that painting there forever,
The crux of the blade and the brush resolved.
When you stand crotched in the ripe deep of things,
As childhood murmurs and the cities call,
Ecstasy wells up from the mixed throes of time.

The Crisis in the Ice Cream

"A hermit who knows what time the trains
Leave," Degas said of Gustave Moreau.
How did he surmise, how did he know
The commonplace in one who took such pains

To be, as he said, "an assembler of dreams"?—
Did he find comfort in a pocket schedule
When fantasy did not conform to rule,
His colors lost in locomotive steams?

That train, that great black dreamer too?—
Any time the picture made him grieve
He could drop the brush, take French leave:
The Côte d'Azur was bluer than his bluest blue.

And orange from oranges, white from sand—
He mainly stayed in Paris though—a trip
Might leave Salome with a bleeding lip:
Nothing travels better than a master hand.

I know, I keep trains waiting in reserve—
An Alpine ice cream, an Italian grape
Alleviate the passion to escape
Unless, of course, I lose my nerve.

The peak drips on the rug, the grapes bleed acid wine,
The orange tastes like diesel fuel.
Moreau, Moreau, contradictions can be cruel—
The Blue Train? Shall I catch it or write another line?

The Lever

When the virile, savage splendor in you
Dies, it is time for the lever, the sea
Touched as if it were a purse full of pearls.
It is time as well to stroke the mountain,
Bathing the finger in its waterfalls,
Choosing its highest peak as a fulcrum
As if the late sky wanted jacking up.
It need not be so big a scale as this:
A needle nestles warm in the haystack,
A pencil pursues its dreams of paper,
The hand on the lip of the lover can
Loose a startlement of amorous phrases,
Lovers lying low almost everywhere—
The letter opener remembers the seal,
And the crowbar is avid for boulders.
Just the slightest movement and you are saved:
The pencil moves on into language,
A rapt lover will never stop talking
Until a kiss invades the rich source of sound
And two nudes at last lie like prime movers.
Therefore, do not cry too much over spilt milk:

It was a slip of the wrist that wanted
A splayed galaxy, or so we must tell
Ourselves, prodding and prodded, here and there—
Chopsticks lust for the rice, and earth listens,
Indulging lovers as its princely pair.

II

Deep Breathing at Midnight

What did the savage think, feel, at sundown:
That he had killed, eaten enough, made love?
Had the blue sea left a scar on his eyes,
A red hibiscus rouged his soul with dust?—
Fully charged, infused, heavy, ripe for sleep.
A glittering star a last spike in the head:
In the morning, a warm, layover man,
Turned on a spit, a plethora of dreams.

You must resist this long ago comrade
At the same time the sea daggers your brain,
And the cosmetic hibiscus primes its puff.
Your hard, bronze body vaunts a scar-proof skin—
A day on the beach assaults your hubris,
You thrill to lashing waves, naked bodies—
The girl with a flower in her hair
Has red, pointed fingernails like stigmas.

So your tough concept of yourself is vain,
Stuck like a porcupine before day's end,
How can you waddle home at sundown?
Star-pursued, who will groom a graceful night?
The savage has not lost his comrade,
And the hammock holds the headwork of years—
Bless the stars, the invasion of percepts,
The pallid soul with its long-lasting glow.

I cannot tell you how often I have
Pulled out the quills and yet kept the punctures,
The bronze body holding a mute shower of spears.
The reason I do not wince and rattle
Is quite simple. The concept has learned one
Lasting trick: Starlight, yes, hot cheeks, brushed lips,
An eyelid closing on a parable.

The Rocking Horse

You may be God's child or quite a little sinner,
But on the horse in the nursery where it all began,
No matter what, you are a winner.

Rocking back and forth, you always win the race
By several lengths to cheering crowds who see
You as a prince of daring, skill, and grace.

Alas, when you come down and touch the floor,
And mother comes in to see what you have been up to,
You begin to learn that winning races consists of something more.

Nowadays it all unfolds before you on the screen,
Luscious girls, fast cars, sumptuous food and wine:
After a while, it comes to look a bit obscene.

The world, it seems, is just an endless track:
Wrecks on the highway, blown-up planes, assassinations—you exit
Onto meadows, mountains, rivers, lakes, but can you really turn
    your back?

Still, since childhoold never really leaves us, we rock and rock and
    rock—
If you are lucky, someone sings a lullaby, someone loves you:
Absorbers instead of sores, when you do not win, take the shock.

Zither

Is it a lazy day, or do your nerves
Feel plucked by anything that's close at hand?—
A rose, a beautiful face, a ripe peach,
Far off, a vista of the brilliant sea,
A kind of willowy command of life,
This way, that way, as if moods were turning
Into meanings, the action of a zither.
The rose may rise to a royal sound,
Or sad, solitary, beauty unnoticed,
The plangent girl pauses in the garden,
And you are picked all over with passion.
The ripe peach doubles as a private sun
Compacted from many glowing mornings.
The sea pulls hardest at the music,
Blue twangs for the rapt, willing wanderer—
And so it is that the actual world
Knows where the instrument lies in the sun,
How the harp of the heart longs to be touched,
How we hold music no one can hear,
The nerve-endings groped through hours of sleep
Restless tumult of things unheard, undone,
Often a kind of sorrowful seaweed,
Hither, thither, the blue submerged reproach.
Some days one is too closed, too comatose,
The invisible plectrum lies flat, silent,
The rose raises no rumor, the ripe peach
Rolls from the sideboard toward the last blackout.
Tongue-kissing the girl will not pick the chord.
One of many, this design of the zither—
That we do not twitch sound when we meet
Means we flutter and flutter inside ourselves,
Waiting for the willowy hand to move.

Pavane for a Dead Parrot

The parrot is dead who lived alone, and spoke against the grain,
Stretched out on the table like a little Indian chief,
Deserted by the tribe and left out in the rain.

Sunless in the kitchen, the landscape through the window full of
    cloud—
Is this what happens speaking to the world in no uncertain
    terms?—
Nothing but a dirty tablecloth to serve as makeshift shroud.

Out there a counter-revolution is blowing on the tattered lawn—
Too late, too late for this stiff, feathered cardboard end:
The cook, clients, children, all the ones he loved and hated, gone.

The storm, no doubt, will overtake the house,
Reclaim the brilliant, cosseted remains, install another chief,
But will he have the heart to make his acid resumés of foolish
    principles, petty laws?

Therefore I wish I had the scattering hand
To pick the feathers up, turn them in an iridescent flame,
And make this final gesture in opposition to the bland.

The gloomy kitchen flares, weird, full of gashes,
As if the cage were the world that tongues are sharpened on—
The hand will go on dreaming of rainbows in the scattered ashes.

The Author of Autumn

As you sit in your chair, waiting for the winds
Of change, one gold leaf falling is a drug
That activates a shimmering sense of grief—
Something so simple, yet powerful—
Your tongue wanting the gold draft of a pill:
A sudden frisson among the hormones—
I am a tissue of autumn, I could
Metastasize the sorrow of nations.

It may well be much more secret than this,
Unknown to your magisterial inertia,
Wishing a flower to stab you in the eye,
The kiss to cut a cicatrice on your face—
A curse plunging in its keen stilletto.
Right now in the calm blood, plans are afoot:
You are always filled with these messengers,
The tight skin a busy mall of minions.

It takes some time and much trial and error,
But you will become adept at footfalls:
Even off season, moods of inlaid grief,
The topaz on her hand milked for torpor,
She, a bearer of autumn in your heart—
Therefore, it is an inner, outer, art—
I have seen the sea, and I contain it:
Sapphire throes or thrombus—what moves today?

Feet run to the sound of the telephone,
The house is a scurrying of agents.
You have hung up on a host of deployers
(Outside, that leaf, beyond, the brilliant wave)
To sit for a while, merely circulate
On the small chance of sieving some brief joy—
One never, never, needs the bitter pill:
It was lodged, coated by a primal sea.

Walking Wounded

Found again, found at last, the oasis is more beautiful, more lush
Because the harsh ring of austerity that surrounds it
Is wider, deeper than I thought, without flower or bush.

In those hot sands it looked like some plump, green, exotic sore—
Could I reach it, could I puncture it, make flowers
Burst forth, the springs, little brook, run once more?

From afar, health can look like sickness, thus
One felt like a tall, dry wound on foot:
Press the swollen earth, and it would run with pus.

Here in the glittering, dazzling, dessicated calm,
I see the man in red pantaloons and fez climbing for dates
As though he made love before he ravished it, the lenient palm.

So I approach with ardor illness and mayhem—
May I break out in flowers, run with the amorous brook,
Among these slack, sleek ambiguities be at last, again one of them.

Yes, yes, the ring is broken, the richness will spill over—
I have walked containment all my life, and loved the desert stain:
I cannot come across the sand as any other kind of lover.

Chameleon

A skull crammed with hyacinths, a pink tomgue
Like the petal of a tulip—that should
Be enough impaction and protrusion
To make the pale morning vehicular—
A turn, a turnaround in a small place.
A phrenologist could feel the blossoms,
The tired doctor with his tongue depressor
Would know they had a case on their hands.

They might wander into fauna, flora,
Ask a chameleon on a white finger
What it can do for a stunning encore:
Perhaps turn harlequin on a green leaf?
The annals of analysis, the rot
That eats at medical imperium—
It is the role of the hyacinth-crammed,
The tulip-tongued, to inspire the lizard.

So I thought that holy, hectic morning
When my own white hand harbored the reptile,
The pink tongue dripping rose wine for tincture.
I think a thought entered the little lion
Who can shock the world with his roving hues.
I cannot quite tell you how exquisite

The day can be when the worn word wallows
In nuance just an inch or two away.

Zebra

The opposition of the world is always here,
Point-blank, in your face, the oath, bruise, crushed limbs:
Do not expect the crocodile to shed a genuine tear.

Almost submerged, one amber eye half-open, he watches yours
    and mine—
The poet waits on the leafy bank of the river:
Don't move until you know exactly how to write that line.

The yellow eye watches in the hazy, golden, city street—
You may have a penthouse, but his sight is long and sharp,
Lurking in the half-suspicious eyes of nearly everyone you meet.

Back to the pale youth on some brilliant day,
Taking notes as zebra, wildebeest, gazelle cross over:
The glistening poem is the one that got away.

Not a mark on it, that arching back, the beautiful striped skin—
It is always a singling out, a majestic reverence if you will:
The bleeding corpse, the thundering herd, private passions
    folding deep within.

It is a decorated, devious way to meet the world, disarm
The memory of jaws that slash and stitch the void:
As long as sunlight lasts, stand at the window and see if golden
    stripes upon your skin have lost their charm.

III

Hemorrhage

Not today, maybe tomorrow, perhaps soon,
You will see your blood lying on the floor, a gored bullfighter's
     fallen cape,
And you will know the meaning of that expression, blood upon the
     moon.

Your life, a thing of shining glory, now torn and disconnected,
And that smeared planet sailing through the sky,
In its ironic way, still pondering the telltale history of the rejected.

But, ah, that shining prince of early days, that matador,
Feeling faint, frightened, as if brushed by a passing orb,
Cannot gather up the clotted folds crumpled on the floor.

If consciousness permits, he still may fantasize
That something sharp but beautiful has almost brought him down,
A broken rainbow in his side, a scimitar of paradise.

A peacock spread of mangled life—
And in that far day, or fairly, nearly here,
He will see that even beauty wields a knife.

More to the point, dial and call the ambulance—
Far across the field, the bull still kicking dust,
And you will know how heavy was the mesh ruptured by the
     rainbow's lance.

Catheter

Did that last peach you ate turn to stone
Or just ferment and change to tumescence?—
Something surely put a tight lid on things
And said to the warm world, no more entrance—
A fig would float up like a silk balloon,
A plum could be a bomb in the bowels:
You feel the aftershocks for hours.

Suddenly now you know the body's shape,
How every meal you eat attacks, forms it:
Some days the intestines slack as hammocks
Because you did not send down the usual,
Needing to make love all night, catch a train.
But, ah, the rebuttal of the banquet,
A symposium of life's resources.

This supine reverie leads to the bed
In the hospital and the catheter,
A man stuffed with jonquils and yellow jade—
Something Oriental as well as Roman
As if one grazed and grazed on lost empires,
The world too shrunken now, too belittled,
The makings of a rich mosaic stored,
Repressed Byzantium of the bladder.

Orange juice through a bent glass straw is a chime,
A reminder if dross should liquefy—
A lust for avid particulars returns,
One simply cannot chide the body further:
You dangle down, touch feet to the golden cubes.
You have been sluiced, tapped, and have tilted up
A mosque of memory the muse inlaid:
Only you know the picture that you had in mind.

Drawing Blood

The blood in the needle longs for land,
Something better than a course of glass,
Where clouds float by and red birds pass:
Man has a topographic hand.

Have you noticed when the finger's pricked
There is a meandering flowing in the brain?
And mounting blood would be off again:
A salty taste of travel on the finger licked.

Of course, oasis calls and calls,
Little streams, rivers, reddish seas.
It may be some inner, outward urge to please
That tints the sunset in the waterfalls.

And then the sharp-billed bird takes part
As if it stuck that vein up in the sky
To drain a thrombus passing by:
A brilliant show of blood calls home the heart.

Bloody, strangled thoughts held in the head,
The closely bandaged finger,
Tell us that source waters linger.
And the bird of night is flying overhead.

It may take something like these little sticking pains
To make us feel we hold in trust
And milk a ruby before we turn to dust;
Oases, streams, sunset rivers, glittering on the plains.

English Walnuts

You crack or open them like a mollusk,
But the meat inside is dry and often looks quite old:
It warns the stranger with a wrinkled, hardened husk.

293

You have a sudden sense of dismembered body parts—
Could it be one pelvis stuck to another, a pair of hips?
Imagination has struck, complex and complicated, into your heart
    of hearts

Where appetite always struggles with concern, disbelief, dismay.
What strange suggestion have you come upon this time?
Is this the first nut of uncertain content you have cracked today?

The yellowed, shrunken pelvis, the long-dismembered hips—
You stroke, almost caress, the mini-things nestled in a grave
Before, cannibal-like, you lift them to your lips.

How long has anything we delve and designate lain
In some dim, random corner? The quartered orange, the blind
    eye of the prune
May raise the age-old specter of murder in the brain.

The marvel is we delve and delve but do not act—
The orange, quartered but not drawn, the prune reminds us of the
    glossy plum:
I eat the loaded kernel, and bless caprice, the long-suffering
    steadiness of fact.

Paperclip

It starts in the unknown, comes back upon
Itself and moves a point into the void.
Someone with the cunning of Daedalus
Made a small metaphysical gesture—
Not so glamorous, heavy, or tight-packed
As the bronze swimmer doubling in the air
As if he silvered inside with some doubt
When the splash of chaos closes the dive.

The paperclip makes a starker, more modest
Claim, and deals in the way of clipped remarks,
Hard-edged and always internalizing—
Cousin to a tense safety pin that keeps

Its mouth shut, but glowers inwardly.
The paperclip means to point, stick no one,
A cool entrail of circularity
As if a winding road hugged itself close.

Those pressured days when we are sorting notes
We may have felt that we have swallowed it,
A crimp in the gut but not a stapler—
Back to the swimmer and his heavy dreams,
That ecstatic tumbling and the splash!
Only a moment. Down on hands and knees,
With fallen hook retrieved between our lips,
We judge the slack of white, recessive sea.

Kangaroo

Ah, the fatigue of it, jumping on two legs—
Isn't it enough to be flatfooted, a glutted sack of weight?—
Should one also have a ludicrous pair of paws that begs?

Perhaps when continents divide, form must gape,
Looking around for some huge cookie cutter to help it out:
A flattened man of gingerbread, perhaps, but not this bounding
    shape.

Just look at that recessive, pushed-back donkey face—
You expect it to hee-haw, to be stubborn, stolid,
And not go flying through the air with, admittedly, amazing grace.

But I, too, have a sense of continents that part,
And have a cookie cutter of my own, just by chance,
Just in case the thing I wanted perfect has a change of heart.

Risen, swollen, like furry dough with something otherwise to say,
It kicks, beats a manic tail against my legs,
And, right beside me, I can hear the donkey bray.

The made-unmade—it wants to beat me up, it wants to box:
I need a pogo stick to go, jumping off, far away—
It will not do to call for gingerbread or pelt the possible with rocks.

Choke Collar

When you have gone too far beyond yourself,
Think of the choke collar, the sudden pull, tug,
As if something measuring travels with you.
When that blue ring you gave her looks diseased,
Ready to slip from her hand in remorse,
When the clock clicks, clacks, talks in pidgin English,
You know time is no longer on your side
Wrapped in the tight tape of the turning day.

Still, that curious little feeling of resolve
As though pullback could release you—
The swaddling cloth of the mummy, the spattered day:
A kilo of blue rushes to the ring,
The phythisic, dropped hand blushes with good health,
The sunlit pool smiles at troubled clocks—
A clear, long view to the stopping-off place,
The entangled figure suddenly turned.

Was it the smell of cooked jewels in the air,
As if old disaster could make new stew?—
The veins flowing with embalming fluid,
The enormous pick-up of all passion
As though fixative oozed from the slowest pace,
That told the dog beside you: Now, yes, now.
We descend—ascend?—to what can mind us:
The scented wind at last has reins in it.

So the day quivers with this quiescence,
Titilating little chains, the worn ropes.
It is uncanny that we sometimes know
That a sick jewel lies on a loved hand,
That the tape is wound to our eyes and mouth,
And the pool is pulsing with repentance.
Any jumble of symbols can rewind:
The loose day is the terror of the hour.

Clean Sweep

The kitchen is so absolutely swept, a confrontational scene:
The sparkling teacups, the kettle, the crouching stove—
Someone has been here with a broom, the stroke was mean.

The table is shining like a little lake of oilcloth,
A surface that excludes the water birds, the rotting rowboat—
The whole house is banked up clean, one knows, no dust, no sloth.

Where are the boots grown muddy on the mountain,
The slicker, steaming, dripping near the stove,
A renegade that seems to say: Where are the orchids and the
    fountain?

Where, indeed, the smell of tracked-in doubt and dung?—
What is this obsessional concern with brushed-off surface
If all the richest odysseys are left unsung?

This dialogue is dangerous, plays it far too fast and loose—
The mind is slit, as though for slides, admit it now, forever,
And pitting kitchen-clean, tabled seas, orchids, fountains, is a bit
    obtuse.

You go home, abraded by the neighbor's brush and broom—
Click. Click. You, too, may harry all the richest pictures
If you do not hold a lover to your heart in an upstairs room.

Cauldron

If you want to jump from the frying pan
Into the fire, remember the cauldron—
A relic nowadays, but once it was used
For boiling dirty clothes, perhaps far back
For men, circled by savages:
That is the caricature of the thing—
Every tool, utensil, a reminder,
A skewer echoes a crusader's lance—

297

The thrill and the throb of the world of things:
The knife that cuts bread a slow guillotine.
Culture and barbarity in the same house,
The mind a nomad, the tent its temple—
The hard odysseys in nails, hammers,
The bruised thumb, hand, mashed with misadventure.
The smoking kettle warns of volcanos:
That tropic land, quiescent caldera.

So we blunder into the iron cauldron
As if we always carry a lode of myths—
Ironic cousin of today's hot tub:
We have come late to basting of ourselves:
Some even make love in the swirled water,
A cauldron of concupiscence,
Lacking only the red volcanic view
As though the tropics had an orgasm.

I saw a huge cauldron once, filled with earth,
Planted with petunias—The bravado
Of the thing enchanted me, small trumpets
Of the inordinate and various:
The black containment, the bright eruption.
I would like to see someone boiling clothes
Again, casual, unconcerned with history
Except those stains that will not wash away.

IV

Cameo

Who was it? Was it the face of Venus?
A forgotten lover known long ago,
Chiseled at the height of some hot passion,
The white face, the background of rusted red,
Mashed, milked from a mass of indecisions?
You can feel the features, cold, harsh to touch.
Is this a small cenotaph on your hand,
Or is the blood still flowing warm somewhere?

As he rowed across the lake, the paddle
Dripped, loose, scattered tears.
He tried to imagine she was still there,
Waiting in the boathouse, dressed in pure white,
With a ruby on her finger, a signal
To him, her seneschal of sensation,
The one who never missed a rendezvous,
Cutting the blue lake like another gem—

Bronzed but still the blue, blue man of her dreams,
Somehow sifted rough-cut in the sieve of fate—
Different shores and different destinations?—
Now rowing alone without cutting edge,
Never to give her the lake as a gift,
Never a blue ring for the other hand.
The rhythm of rowing is self-righteous,
Yet tearful, himself an upright carving.

Almost no one wears cameos anymore,
Memorialization lost in the fast lane.
But his hand is heavy, the stilled picture
Hard to lift from the lake as a stone.
I count his crossings, recrossings, mine,
I can smell the dried blood in the setting.
I spend my life defining, refining,
Rubbing the cameo for throbbing print.

The Etymologist in the Orchard

When was a peach first called a peach?
How did it slowly ripen in the sun
Before you read it in the lexicon?
What are the flesh and pit of speech?

Words have been my passion—it seems like ages—
My eyes, my lips, my tongue,
May never know just how the fruit hung
In the sun fell among the printed pages.

I love the fruit itself, and still want more—
What glorious savage felt the round
Delicious thing and uttered sound?—
I want the surface of the world, I want the core.

I like to think the luscious, uttered sound revealed
That something flowered, ripened in the grunt,
And language soared above the tribal hunt,
Fell back again, of course, to spear and shield.

Those black eyes, painted faces, dancing feet—
The dictionary is a beating drum
To let the world go free and bring it home:
The thing itself, the word, conjoin, disjoin, compete.

The drum is still, the peach impeaches
Any name that has not felt the savage lip.

The dust, the blood, the final savor of the trip:
What the world withholds, and what it teaches.

The Idea in the Garden

He was a man of intense desires and needs—
The garden was well-kept, the goldfish pool immaculate,
But somehow the water clouded, the garden choked with weeds.

All because he was for some time ill—
Recovery was slow, things got out of hand:
His Idea of the world was not supported by his Will.

He let it go, reduced the concepts of a little god.
Summer aged, the phlox, his scepters, ruined by revolution
When what had looked like weeds became the goldenrod.

The impeccable overrun by dissidents, but this was left,
After all in ruin a striking moral note
As if the underworld decreed: Wounded, yes, but not totally bereft.

Even dusty summers, dying stalk by stalk,
Will not go down dishonored by the underworld:
These golden banners wave above the catafalque.

It takes a while for all immaculates to understand,
To feel the golden tremor underground,
How every garden willed is ruled by countermand.

An Epistemological Incident

What is the meaning of insight?—
Just a book's illuminating page,
Or just a singular image
Of a crow perched against the moonlight?

An entrail drawn through the old dark town.
Nothing is more ecstatic than the trail
Of an image as it plies its own way:
At sundown, the dropped thread, the red snapback—
The swans honking below the castle wall.

The Work of the Sun

Verlaine said the poem rises slowly like the sun,
Spreads over the landscape, a bird that hovers,
Moves on to find and bless a pair of lovers:
The work of the sun is never done.

It loves the still, ardent, and the physical—
The house is closed—it climbs the stair,
And leaves its shaded footprints everywhere:
The always prowling word is never finical.

A vast impressionist, it mixes palettes—
You think you have the sunlight captured on a nude,
But it never meant to stay too long or brood—
Clouds pass by, and in a moment it forgets.

It dawdles with the minatory and the minuscule,
Spotlights a hidden bruise, a scar beneath the brim:
Someone beaten, slashed—Her or Him?
A realist as well, it does not join with any school.

Random rover, it wants to get most things just right—
Some days I feel it heating liquid in my pen,
The sunlit river flows a while and then
Lovers leave my land, an evening bird takes flight.

After all, the magnum opus came to grips
With crimes of passion, soft caresses,
Things picked out by starlight which it barely blesses:
Something put a hand upon the sun and sealed its lips.